$\mathcal{U}$nveiling
the
SECRET LIFE
of BEES

POPULAR INSIGHTS

Solving the Da Vinci Code Mystery
Brandon Gilvin

Wisdom from the Five People You Meet in Heaven
Brandon Gilvin and Heather Godsey

Unveiling the Secret Life of Bees
Amy Lignitz Harken

$\mathcal{U}$nveiling
the
SECRET LIFE
of BEES

AMY LIGNITZ HARKEN

CHALICE
PRESS
ST. LOUIS, MISSOURI

Biblical quotations, unless otherwise noted, are from the *New Revised Standard Version Bible,* copyright 1989, Division of Christian Education of the National Council of the Churches of Christ in the United States of America. Used by permission. All rights reserved.

Those quotations marked RSV are from the *Revised Standard Version of the Bible,* copyright 1952, [2nd edition, 1971] by the Division of Christian Education of the National Council of the Churches of Christ in the United States of America. Used by permission. All rights reserved.

Scripture quotations marked (NIV) are taken from the HOLY BIBLE, NEW INTERNATIONAL VERSION®. NIV®. Copyright © 1973, 1978, 1984 by International Bible Society. Used by permission of Zondervan Publishing House. All rights reserved.

Scripture quotations marked (TEV) are taken from the *Today's English Version*— Second Edition © 1992 by American Bible Society. Used by permission.

Page numbers in this edition refer to the hardcover edition of *The Secret Life of Bees,* published by Viking Penguin in 2002, and may differ slightly from page numbers of the paperback edition published by Penguin Books in 2003.

Cover and interior design: Elizabeth Wright

This book is printed on acid-free, recycled paper.

Visit Chalice Press on the World Wide Web at
www.chalicepress.com

10 9 8 7 6 5 4 3 2 1   05   06   07   08   09

Library of Congress Cataloging–in–Publication Data

Harken, Amy Lignitz.
  Unveiling the secret life of bees / Amy Lignitz Harken.
    p. cm. — (Popular insights)
  ISBN 13: 978-0-827230-26-5 (pbk. : alk. paper)
  ISBN 10: 0-827230-26-5
  1. Kidd, Sue Monk. Secret life of bees. 2. Christian fiction, American—History and criticism. 3. Women in literature. 4. Girls in literature. I. Title. II. Series.
  PS3611.I44S383 2005
  813'.54—dc22

                                                                2004030147

Printed in the United States of America

To Jane E. McAvoy (1957–2004)

Contents

Introduction

Unless you're deathly afraid of or allergic to bees, the hum of a bee can be a thing of comfort, particularly after reading Sue Monk Kidd's novel *The Secret Life of Bees*.

Throughout the novel, the winged insects buzz in and around each character. They portend both life and death, signal both divine and earthly companionship, and urge some characters to new life while holding others to the stable life they treasure. In a way, Kidd's bees are like the biblical Paraclete—the Counselor, the Holy Spirit: constant, ever-responsive to human need.

You might read this novel as a "coming of age" novel. Lily, a white, motherless fourteen-year-old girl, escapes a dull and difficult life with a hard and difficult father by running away to Tiburon, South Carolina. As Lily sets out on her quest of liberation and renewal, she takes with her Rosaleen, an African American woman who has been a stand-in caretaker since Lily was four, when Lily's birth mother died in an accidental shooting. Given Lily's age and spiritual awakening, *The Secret*

Life of Bees is indeed about growing up and coming into one's own. You might notice her budding sexuality, her increasing awareness of the Divine, and her happy (eventually) inclusion in a group of women who draw strength from one another.

As Lily and Rosaleen find themselves in the embrace of the "calendar sisters"—August, May, and June—other themes emerge, including the theme of presence. The novel is about divine presence and how we experience it, and about the presence of others and how salvation can be found there as well.

Kidd's book is about the divine, about religion, and about invocation. It might challenge the way you think about God. Instead of a male Father God, which many Christians find familiar, even comforting, Kidd's book revolves around the spirit of Mary, the mother of Jesus. Yet this book is not primarily concerned with Mary's role as Jesus' mother. Instead the focus is on Mary as a protector and guardian, Mary as the face of God, Mary as the mother of us all, Mary as the long-sufferer who understands all woe.

Although *The Secret Life of Bees* emphasizes Mary's presence in times of woe and in our own hearts, the sense of presence cannot be located in her alone. Characters are very much involved in the practice of being with one another, and absences are well noted. This book is as much about the human community as it is about communion with the Divine. Rosaleen is present for Lily while her mother is absent and her father emotionally absent. The calendar sisters are present for one another, and May's eventual physical absence is deeply felt. Lily and August are present for Zach in his crisis. Even Neil, who vows never to return to the Boatwright household after a fight with June, is present for the crisis of Zach's arrest.

A delightful thing about novels such as Kidd's is that each reader brings his or her own heart and mind to the text and so discerns individual messages and inspirations. Other ideas that run throughout the book may have captured your interest, including remembrance, forgiveness, reconciliation, race relations, or liberation. No study guide can be comprehensive, but in this guide we will attempt to explore a number of themes. As this guide is aimed for the most part at Christian readers, many of the themes explored will be related to the church.

Kidd's book takes its title from the various roles that bees play within the hive:

> "Most people don't have any idea about all the complicated life going on inside a hive. Bees have a secret life we don't know anything about."
>
> I loved the idea of bees having a secret life, just like the one I was living.
>
> "What other secrets have they got?" I wanted to know.
>
> "Well, for instance, every bee has its role to play."
>
> (*Bees,* 148)

Just as bees have their own specialized roles to play in the creation of honey, so women have their own roles in society and families. Accordingly, this book will be organized along the lines of women's roles: sister, wife, and so on. In exploring these roles, we will highlight women from the Bible and also characters from *The Secret Life of Bees.* Our exploration will include information about the history of the church, social contexts for biblical writings, and open questions that today's faithful hold.

Because the spirit of Mary pervades the novel and because Mary remains a mystery to many Protestant readers, we will begin with a close look at the mother of Jesus. In the novel the role of "Divine Mother" is symbolized by a wooden Madonna figure. This figure is such a central symbol in the novel that she takes on the qualities of a "character." The three-foot wooden carving is an object of veneration for the calendar sisters and their religious community, the Daughters of Mary. The black Mary opens the door to issues of liberation and oppression.

We will look at how the Virgin Mary has been perceived around the world as a symbol of divine presence in times of suffering and oppression, and as inspiration for spiritual resistance.

In chapter 2 the "Divine Mother" becomes the "Earth Mother," as seen through the character of Rosaleen. In this chapter, we will look at the importance of not just a symbolic, remote divine source, but of incarnation, an earthly divine presence. In the novel Rosaleen is often the character who brings issues to the fore and forces others to take a stand. Because Rosaleen is an African American living in a Caucasian world, examining her role will also allow us to look at the issue of racism, including the issue of African American surrogate mother figures.

Much of this novel revolves around rituals—sacred rituals, personal religions, and impromptu sacraments. Some rituals in the novel are communal, such as the Mary-centered Sunday morning worship services. Other rituals are purely individual, such as the mother-centered shrines Rosaleen and Lily each construct. Chapter 3, "Sister," explores the ideas of sacrament and ritual through the character of May, who suffered an emotional blow many years prior and remains unable to cope with the troubles of the world. May ritualistically retreats to her stone "wailing wall," into whose crevices she tucks the worries that she pencils onto paper. Through May we explore issues of religion and religious expression and look at the creation of new or private rituals when existing religions are not adequate.

After the groundwork of the first three chapters, the final three chapters look more pointedly at specific characters. In chapter 4, "Daughter," we spend some time with Lily. Although Lily's experience in this novel has often been described as transformation, we look at her story as one of rebirth. Besides allowing us to explore the issues of memory and forgiveness, taking the point of view of Lily's rebirth lets us look at one particular ritual, baptism.

Chapter 5, "Queen," presents the opportunity to examine one of the novel's most interesting characters. August, the "queen bee" in this story, is arguably the strongest female character in the novel. And yet she is not invincible, and she depends on the support of her family and friends. The primary issues in this chapter will be those of community and leadership.

Finally, we look at the role of "Wife," as seen through the lens of Lily's dead mother, Deborah Fontanel Owens. As this is the only female title that takes its identity by its relation to a male, this chapter will be used to explore the male-female relationships in this novel, including those of Lily and Zach and of June and Neil.

Underlying this study a few questions pervade:

How do we connect with God?

To what degree is it necessary and/or appropriate for women to find alternative modes of religion and expressions of faith when they consider traditional modes inadequate or oppressive?

How do we identify legitimate religious expression and worship, ensuring that we are not creating God in our own image?

While this study guide is intended to provoke an examination of these and other questions, it is not intended to give definitive answers. Just as each man and woman brings his and her own heart, mind, and soul to a novel, each must find ways to bring his or her whole being before God. We hope this guide will be a starting point for groups and individuals to explore their own relationships with God. May we always be open to discover new ways to connect with God, whether in the hymns of our foremothers and forefathers, ancient rituals and sacraments of the church, a holy gathering of spiritual siblings, or in a private moment in a meadow. Surely the mystery of God is large enough to encompass the array of human experience, as our souls reach for communion with the One who gave us life, who loves us, and wishes most of all to draw us close.

CHAPTER 1

Divine Mother
THE BLACK MARY'S STRENGTH

"Blessed are you among women, and blessed is the fruit of your womb…And blessed is she who believed that there would be a fulfillment of what was spoken to her by the Lord."

(Lk. 1:42–45)

She was a mix of mighty and humble all in one. I didn't know what to think, but what I felt was magnetic and so big it ached like the moon had entered my chest and filled it up…

I wanted to cry, but then in the next instant, I wanted to laugh, because the statue also made me feel like Lily the Smiled-Upon, like there was goodness and beauty in me, too. Like I really had all that fine potential Mrs. Henry said I did.

Standing there, I loved myself and I hated myself. That's what the black Mary did to me, made me feel my glory and my shame at the same time.

(*Bees*, 70–71)

With hand raised in a fist, the wooden black Mary stands in a corner of the calendar sisters' parlor. She is welcoming, yet defiant; beautiful, yet worn and imperfect. She is a symbol of strength, yet she conveys empathy toward the vulnerable. In the Boatwright household, worship, faith, and life itself swirl around the statue's gnarled countenance in such a way that she becomes more than just a decorative carving. She is a silent participant, an observer. Without words, she can prod, encourage, challenge, and prompt memory in all the humans who come under her gaze.

The statue and the woman she represents provide a constant presence in *The Secret Life of Bees.* Not only is the statue physically present for the goings on in the life of the Boatwright household, but Mary, the mother of Jesus, is invoked throughout the novel, particularly in times of crisis. Mary not only hovers in the background of the novel. She provides its spiritual foundation, and for this reason, we begin our discussion of the novel with a look at Mary, including her portrayals in the Bible, in church tradition, and in society.

Mary is an ambiguous figure. She is both a mother and a virgin. She is both intensely human and yet bearer of the Divine. She is a historical figure, and yet history—outside the Bible— has little to say about her. Instead she is wrapped in centuries of tradition that ascribe to her events and characteristics that have no biblical testimony.

Generations of Christians have found studying and understanding Mary both a difficult and an exhilarating task. The Catholic Church has long discussed and debated Mary's participation in the process of redemption. In recent decades Protestants have come to appreciate her more fully. Feminist theologians have embraced Mary as a way for women to recognize a feminine expression of the Divine. As August tells Lily, "everybody needs a God who looks like them" (141). Likewise cultures all over the world have come to see Mary as a symbol of God's preference for the poor.

The black Mary is such a symbol in *The Secret Life of Bees*. Many generations before Lily came to the Boatwright household, a slave had found the black Mary washed up on the shore. The slaves adopted her as a religious icon, recognizing in her so much of what they saw in themselves: dark skin, a watery journey to South Carolina, experience and empathy with the sorrows of the world. The black Mary passed through generations of slaves until she wound up in the possession of August and her sisters.

For the calendar sisters and the other Daughters of Mary, the black Mary represents many things. They believe that she can help and empower them. She is a source of celebration: around her they celebrate their own ritual of the Feast of the Assumption, incorporating their own special thanksgiving for the honey crop.

And in this ritual they also celebrate Mary's ability to liberate people from not only physical bondage but also spiritual, social, and emotional bondage. She also symbolizes divine power within. Perhaps you found your own meanings in the statue of the black Mary.

Many Portraits: Mary in the Bible

Lily, who attends a Baptist church, admits her ignorance about Mary, associating her with Catholics, who, according to her minister, are bound for hell.

> The only Mary story we talked about was the wedding story—the time she persuaded her son, practically against his will, to manufacture wine in the kitchen out of plain water. This had been a shock for me, since our church didn't believe in wine or, for that matter, in women having a lot of say about things. (*Bees*, 58)

The Bible contains much more about Mary than the account in John's gospel of Jesus' first miracle at the wedding in Cana. But outside of the four gospels, we don't find much.

The book of Revelation contains a visionary account of a woman giving birth to one who will be a Christ figure, but she is never named as "Mary," and the connection to Mary seems tenuous. That woman is better seen as the church bringing forth the Messiah. The apostle Paul gave us the earliest biblical account of Mary, as his letter to the Galatians was written probably in the early 50s C.E., earlier than even the gospels. But he never names her. He only reports that Jesus was "born of a woman" (Gal. 4:4). In the book of Acts, written by the author of Luke's gospel, Mary is named among those gathered with the disciples in Jerusalem following Jesus' death and resurrection (Acts 1:14).

Most of what we know about Mary comes from the gospels. While it is tempting to combine the accounts of Mary into one unified portrait, note that each gospel paints a different picture of her.

The gospel of Mark, the gospel written earliest, gives the skimpiest account of Mary. In Mark's third chapter, people are saying that Jesus is insane or possessed by demons. Mary and Jesus' brothers come to Jesus. Told that his mother and brothers are asking for him, Jesus claims that his disciples and those who do the will of God are his family (Mk. 3:31–35). In a sense, he disowns Mary and his brothers.

The gospel of Matthew gives us one of two accounts of Jesus' birth (Luke gives us the other, and it is very different). In Matthew's gospel, Mary is fairly passive; Joseph is the more significant parent. Jesus could trace his Davidic ancestry through Joseph—an important connection that tied Jesus to Old Testament messianic prophecy. (Luke also traced the Davidic line through Joseph.) An angel appears to Joseph three times. The first time, the angel urges Joseph not to follow his inclination to divorce Mary (1:19–23). The angel later returns to tell Joseph to take his family and flee to Egypt (2:13). On the third visit, the angel tells Joseph to go back home (2:20). Mary, in Matthew's account, has no voice and no opinion.

The gospel of Luke gives us the fullest, most favorable picture of Mary, portraying Mary as the more important parent in the story of Jesus' birth. The angel Gabriel announces Mary's pregnancy (the annunciation, Lk. 1:26–38) to Mary. Mary makes the decision to consent to God's will (1:38). Further, Mary takes it upon herself to visit her cousin Elizabeth, stay with her for a time, and then return home. During this visit she utters the now-famous and much beloved words of the "Magnificat," so named from the first word of the Latin translation. The hopeful words (1:46–55) have made Mary an inspiration for the poor and oppressed around the world. Nowhere in this story does Mary ask for Joseph's opinion or consent.

Unlike in Matthew's gospel, Mary's pregnant condition is never presented in Luke as a reason for divorce or abandonment. Further, when Mary and Joseph take the baby Jesus to the temple for dedication, Simeon, a devout man there, addresses Mary directly (2:34–35). Finally, twelve years later, when Mary and Joseph find Jesus with the teachers in the temple, Mary, not Joseph, addresses her son (2:48). In Luke's gospel, Mary is an independent, active agent who works in partnership with God. Luke's Mary, unlike the Mary of Mark and Matthew, has a personality. She consents to God's will, but only after questioning the enormity of the situation (1:29, 34). Mary is not merely a passive observer. She ponders and treasures "all these things in her heart" (2:19, 51).

The gospel of John gives us perhaps the fullest understanding of Mary as a disciple of Jesus (i.e., Jn. 2:12), with her prominent presence at two crucial points. Matthew and Luke are silent about Mary during Jesus' adult ministry, and Mark's gospel undercuts Mary's position in favor of the twelve disciples and later followers of Jesus. But John gives us two accounts of Mary as a faithful disciple and active participant in Jesus' ministry. John never uses her name, referring to her only as Jesus' mother. At the wedding at Cana in Galilee

(Jn. 2:1–11), Mary prods Jesus into action after the party runs out of wine, and further instructs the disciples to follow Jesus' orders. Mary notices the negative situation and takes steps to correct it, bringing about the first of Jesus' miracles and subsequent belief by his disciples.

Scholars strongly debate Jesus' reply to Mary in John 2:4: "Woman, what concern is that to you and to me?" (NRSV). Various versions of the Bible give various translations, each of which puts a different spin on Jesus' words, from "O woman, what have you to do with me?" (RSV) to "Dear woman, why do you involve me?" (NIV), to "You must not tell me what to do" (TEV). Literally, the translation is "What is to me and to you, woman?" While scholars ascribe varying degrees of harshness to Jesus' reply, we find no reason to interpret it as rude. Today if a man were to address a woman as "woman!" without using her name, we might see that as being disrespectful or abrupt. But that wasn't the case in Jesus' time. It is far more likely that Jesus is calling Mary "woman" as a sign of respect and honor. We do note Jesus' concern about the timeliness of his being revealed as the messiah. Perhaps that is the thrust of his lament, as he looks toward not only his ministry but also his violent death. Mary's statement about the wine is entirely appropriate, and Jesus takes the action as his mother has alerted him.

The second account takes us to the cross, where we find Mary standing with her sister and Mary Magdalene (Jn. 19:25–27). All four gospels mention women at the foot of the cross, but only in John's gospel do we find Jesus' mother listed specifically. Here, just moments before his death, Jesus turns Mary over to the care of the "disciple whom he loved," another unnamed character.

Mary in *Bees:* "Our Lady of Chains"

While Lily doesn't know much about the Mary of the Bible and while the carved figurehead looks nothing like images of Mary she's seen, Lily instantly recognizes the wooden statue in the Boatwright parlor as Mary. Likewise, Lily's description of the carving bears little resemblance to images we often see of Mary. The art tradition of Europe has typically portrayed Mary as possessing the features of a classic white beauty. She is generally submissive, maternal, prayerful—especially in portrayals of the annunciation. Her facial expression either bears sorrow over the loss of her son, or a peaceful, inviting countenance.

The black Mary in the parlor is twisted, gnarled, and holding a fist up in defiance. She was given the title "Our Lady of Chains" as a moniker of liberation.

> The room grew quiet as August stood there a minute, letting everything sink in. When she spoke again, she raised her arms out beside her. "The people called her Our Lady of Chains. They called her that not because she *wore* chains…"
>
> "*Not because she wore chains,*" the Daughters chanted.
>
> "They called her Our Lady of Chains because *she broke them.*" (*Bees*, 110)

Just as the slaves in pre-Civil War South Carolina found the black Mary a source of understanding and liberation, so the Daughters of Mary find her a source of strength and determination in their circumstances: the turbulent, frightening peak of the civil rights movement in the South.

But the black Mary is many other things for the Daughters of Mary as well. She is the object of their gratitude for the honey crop; she is the central figure of their Sunday worship; she is the main character during the celebration of the Feast of the Assumption.

Protestants in particular might be unnerved or disturbed that a wooden figure washed ashore would be an object of veneration for the Daughters of Mary. Protestants have long had reservations about veneration of statues, which are much more common in Roman Catholic churches. Seeing Catholics kneel before statues, some Protestants have accused the church of promoting idol worship.

The Catholic Church understands statues to represent people who bear God's holiness. The statues are expressions of faith by those who create them and for those who use them as devotional objects. The veneration is aimed not toward the statue itself, but to the one it represents. A person kneeling before a statue of Mary is honoring the person of Mary, who bears the holiness of God, not the statue.

The spirit Mary is also called on in *The Secret Life of Bees,* especially in times of crisis. Note how many times Lily and August utter her name or look at her picture for strength or guidance. Further, August adds another dimension—Mary is the Divine within:

> "Our Lady is not some magical being out there some-
> where, like a fairy godmother. She's not in the statue in
> the parlor. She's something *inside* of you." (*Bees,* 288)

People who hold special reverence for Mary the mother of Jesus find a mix of qualities in her. As the "Mother of God," she contains aspects of the Divine. Yet the historical Mary was but a simple peasant girl, presumably with all the pains and sorrows that we all carry. Tradition (which developed over the centuries after the Bible found its final form) holds that Mary was assumed bodily into heaven, just as Jesus was. In heaven she is in a unique position to help with human woes. With a human mother's care, she understands our problems. With a mother's influence, she can mediate our worries and guilt to Jesus. That is, she is the "mediator with the Mediator." Although the Bible doesn't say much about Mary, over the centuries the church's understanding of her has emerged and evolved.

Mary in the Church

Much scholarly work has been done to find out about "the historical Jesus," that is, what can be confirmed about the person of Jesus of Nazareth from sources outside the Bible. This study is possible because some historians of Jesus' time and shortly thereafter wrote about him. Unfortunately, we don't have such luck with the "historical Mary." The sources simply don't exist.

Tradition, however, has added to the Mary story things that some Christians understand and believe about her without historical or biblical evidence.

The first generations of Christians did not have much to say about Mary. Beginning in the mid-second century, they came to understand her in three ways. First, she was the "New Eve." While Eve disobeyed God (Gen. 3) by eating the fruit from the Tree of the Knowledge of Good and Evil, Mary obeyed God's will, agreeing to bear the baby Jesus (Lk. 1:38). This line of thought began with Justin Martyr, who died in the year 165. While the serpent deceived Eve, Mary was a faithful believer. In fact, many call her the first believer. Some people further understand Mary to be the "mother" of the entire Christian church.

Second, the church came to believe in her "perpetual virginity." Not only was Mary a virgin when she conceived, but she remained a virgin throughout her life. This did not go uncontested. One of the church fathers, Tertullian, assumed that the brothers and sisters of Jesus mentioned in the Bible were children of Mary and Joseph. Other church leaders interpreted the reference to siblings to mean cousins, or they believed that Joseph was actually a widower who had children from a previous marriage. The virginity of Mary is still a matter of debate, even including whether she was a virgin when she conceived Jesus.

Third, the church came to understand Mary as the "Mother of God." This concept also came with a bit of controversy. In the fifth century, some leaders said the church could call her the "Mother of Christ" because she gave birth to Jesus in human form, but not in his Divinity. The church decided that as Jesus was but one person, in whom were mingled Divine and human, they could appropriately call Mary the "Mother of God."

In the Middle Ages, church thought about Mary continued to develop. She came to be seen as a mediator between sinners and God's grace. Part of this has to do with a medieval theology in which Jesus was understood to be a stern judge, ready to condemn sinful human beings to fiery hell. Mary came to represent mercy, a human person who could take human anxieties and human sin and mediate them before Christ. Today many Catholics and Protestants alike understand that Mary is present and active in the church, and through the church she is present and active in our salvation.

The Catholic Church teaches four major doctrines about Mary. We have talked about two: her perpetual virginity (before, during, and after the birth of Christ) and her divine maternity ("Mother of God"). The two others are relatively new. The doctrine of Immaculate Conception holds that Mary was conceived without original sin. This concept began in the Middle Ages, but was declared a dogma by a papal degree only in 1854. The doctrine of the Assumption holds that Mary was taken up—body and soul—into heaven when she died.

More about the Assumption

The Secret Life of Bees is not concerned about Mary's virginity. The Daughters of Mary were not in awe of Mary's obedience to God, nor of the fact that she bore the Christ. Mary's assumption into heaven, however, was reason to celebrate. On August 15, Lily wakes to find the calendar sisters busily preparing for "Mary Day."

> "A thousand years ago women were doing this exact same thing," said August. "Baking cakes for Mary on her feast day."
>
> June looked at my blank face. "Today is the Feast of the Assumption. August fifteenth. Don't tell me you never heard of that."

Oh, sure, the Feast of the Assumption—Brother Gerald preached on that every other Sunday. Of course I'd never heard of it. I shook my head. "We didn't really allow Mary at our church except at Christmas."

August smiled and dunked a wooden drizzle into the vat of honey, which sat on the counter by the toaster oven. While she spun honey across the tops of a fresh pan of cakes, she explained to me in detail how the Assumption was nothing less than Mary rising up to heaven. Mary died and woke up, and the angels carried her up there in swirling clouds. (*Bees,* 220f.)

Lily is like many Protestants, knowing very little about traditions surrounding Mary beyond her giving birth to Jesus in a stable on Christmas Eve. Mary's assumption into heaven is not attested to in the Bible, though literature written at about the same time as some New Testament documents give two versions of Mary's death and afterlife. In one story, Mary's body is resurrected by Jesus after she dies, and it is carried up into heaven.

Belief in Mary's assumption first appeared in the sixth century, possibly in Egypt. By the mid-seventh century, Mary's main feast day became a celebration of her bodily assumption into heaven. Teaching of the Assumption dates back to ancient times but was declared a dogma only in 1950.

Mary in Society

When May goes missing in the novel, her worried sisters, Lily, and Rosaleen search for her. As they make their way along the riverbank in the moonlight, Lily begins to pray aloud. Lily does not pray the Lord's Prayer (the Our Father); rather, she prays the Hail Mary.

Later, when August explains to Lily that she carries within her a constant source of strength, August is not referring to the Holy Spirit or Jesus, but to Mary. "This Mary I'm talking about sits in your heart all day long, saying, 'Lily you are my everlasting home. Don't you ever be afraid. I am enough. We are enough'" (289). Those words come back to Lily at the climax of the story and give Lily wisdom and insight to know what to do, and the strength to do it. Note how many times in the novel Lily pulls out the Mary icon for strength and inspiration.

The slaves adopted the black Mary carving as a religious figure precisely because they believed she could identify with their suffering:

> "Everyone knew the mother of Jesus was named Mary, and that she'd seen suffering of every kind. That she was strong and constant and had a mother's heart. And here she was, sent to them on the same waters that had brought them here in chains. It seemed to them she knew everything they suffered." (*Bees,* 109)

While the church and biblical scholars have debated Mary's virginity, Assumption, and Immaculate Conception, for the poor and oppressed peoples of the world Mary has stood as an inspiration and comfort. She is a divine mother, a protector, a symbol of resistance and strength.

From her words from Luke in the Magnificat, we know she considered herself to be poor:

> "For he has looked with favor on
> > the lowliness of his servant...
> He has shown strength with his arm;
> > he has scattered the proud in the thoughts of their hearts,
> He has brought down the powerful from their thrones,
> > and lifted up the lowly;
> he has filled the hungry with good things,
> > and sent the rich away empty."
>
> (Lk. 1:48–53)

Not only does Mary recognize her own "lowliness," but she announces to the world that God reverses fortunes: the poor and hungry, that is, the oppressed, are satisfied; the rich and powerful, that is, the oppressors, are brought down. Mary continues to be a voice of justice.

Latin American cultures in particular hold special regard for Mary. She was the patron saint of the Conquistadors— the Spanish conquerors of Latin America—and they introduced her to the indigenous peoples. The indigenous peoples, however, did not want to give up their own divinities. Then, on December 9, 1531, an Aztec Indian named Juan Diego beheld an apparition of Mary. She spoke to him in his native language. When the bishop asked for proof, Mary sent Juan Diego to the top of a hill, where he discovered roses growing. He collected the roses in his cloak to take back to the bishop as proof. Upon opening his cloak before the bishop, he discovered an image of Mary. Our Lady of Guadalupe, as she has been called, is now the patron saint of all the Americas and serves as a mother figure for Latin American people.

This is not the only time that Mary has appeared to a common, poor person:

- In 1846 she appeared to two young cattle herders in La Salette, France.
- In 1858, she appeared to a young French girl, Bernadette, in Lourdes, France.
- In 1917 she appeared to young Portugese shepherds in Fatima.

Other claims of apparitions include Mary's reported appearances since 1981 to six children in Medjugorje, in the former Yugoslavia. Not only has Mary brought comfort and hope, but legends also report of Mary's divine protection, mercy, guidance, and miraculous healings.

As Mary has represented a sign of liberation for some oppressed cultures, others, particularly those in male-dominated societies, have felt shackled by the ambivalence about her being both a virgin and a mother. Where the Blessed Virgin is venerated, a high value is placed on a woman's sexual inexperience. Yet male dominance also requires women to be sexual. It leaves women in a quandary: if they are to be like Mary, are they to remain virginal yet also bear children?

Mary: The Feminine Aspect of God?

The Secret Life of Bees is a spiritual novel, concerned with how the Divine is manifest in the lives of Lily, Rosaleen, the calendar sisters, and all the other characters. The novel places the Divine spirit and source almost exclusively in the person of Mary.

Some Protestants, particularly women, have complained that Protestantism has handed them a tradition that is too male dominated: God is always a "father," and Jesus, of course, is male. Many strong female figures in the Bible are ignored, or downplayed. There is, among some Protestants, almost a "Mary envy" of the Catholic faith, which uplifts Mary and other female saints.

In this way, Kidd's novel provides us with something that is not readily apparent in the Bible or perhaps in our church or religious life. Kidd gives us a picture of the feminine aspects of the Divine, and we hope it will help women recognize and appreciate the divine spirit within themselves.

Yet for Christian readers, it is fair to recognize that Jesus himself is mostly missing from *The Secret Life of Bees*. Where the name of Jesus is mentioned, it is most likely to be in the form of an expletive.

Much of what church tradition has come to understand and believe about Mary has everything to do with what the church understands and believes about the person of Jesus. This includes Mary's assumption into heaven, Mary's mysterious participation or presence in our salvation, and the beautiful words of the Magnificat. We might ask ourselves how far we can go in our relationship with Mary without acknowledging her role as the mother of Jesus. That question need not detract from the appropriateness of finding Mary a legitimate source of strength and inspiration.

When August tells Lily that it is important that people have a God who looks like they do, she is referring to African Americans being able to see themselves in representations of God. This is true not just across races, but across genders. We are all made in God's image. We can not only appreciate ourselves as creatures of God, but know that there is nothing about us, be it our sex or race, that alienates us from God, in all God's manifestations.

QUESTIONS FOR DISCUSSION

1. What do you think the black Mary represents in the novel? In what characters does she represent liberation, and how does she represent that?

2. Protestants, going back to the Reformation of the Middle Ages, have criticized devotion to Mary and the dogmas declared about her by the church. Part of the concern was that she drew attention away from our worship of God and our reliance on Jesus. Yet some believe that Protestantism has not done enough to hold up prominent women in the story of Christianity. Do you feel Protestantism needs more female examples of strength and/or piety? Is Mary the proper one to provide this?

3. How does the black Mary carving resemble the biblical Mary? How does she differ? Does reading biblical accounts of Mary, the mother of Jesus, shed light on your understanding on the role of "Our Lady of Chains" in the lives of the Daughters of Mary?

4. The slave population and the Daughters of Mary identified the black Mary as a religious icon because they felt she

could identify with them. Lily thinks that it is more important that Mary be able to understand her than for Mary to be perfect. Is it more important to you to believe that God can sympathize with your problems, or that God can help you out of your problems (even if God is too powerful to be able to relate firsthand).

5. What attributes that tradition ascribes to Mary are also ascribed to Jesus? Do you think the Daughters of Mary substitute Mary for Jesus in their religious life? In what ways is this appropriate? In what ways is it inappropriate?

FURTHER READING

Carl E. Braaten and Robert W. Jenson, eds., *Mary, Mother of God*. Grand Rapids: Eerdmans, 2004.

Sandra Cisneros, *The House on Mango Street*. Houston: Arte Publico Press, 1983.

Ivone Gebara and Maria Clara Bingemer, *Mary: Mother of God, Mother of the Poor*. Maryknoll, N.Y.: Orbis, 1989.

Elizabeth A. Johnson, *Truly Our Sister*. New York: Continuum, 2003.

Rosemary Radford Ruether, *Mary—The Feminine Face of the Church*. Philadelphia: Westminster Press, 1977.

CHAPTER 2

Earthly Mother
ROSALEEN'S JUSTICE

"His mercy is for those who fear him
  from generation to generation.
He has shown strength with his arm;
  he has scattered the proud in the thoughts of their hearts.
He has brought down the powerful from their thrones,
  and lifted up the lowly;
he has filled the hungry with good things,
  and sent the rich away empty."

(Lk. 1:50–53)

This is the autumn of wonders, yet every day, every single day, I go back to that burned afternoon in August when T. Ray left. I go back to that one moment when I stood in the driveway with small rocks and clumps of dirt around my feet and looked back at the porch. And there they were. All these mothers. I have more mothers than any eight girls off the street. They are the moons shining over me.

(*Bees*, 302)

Think *mother* and what comes to mind?

Is it the ever-giving mother characterized by the old standard "M-O-T-H-E-R," in which the *M* stands for the "million things she gave me," the *T* for "tears were shed to save me," *H* for "heart of purest gold" and the *R* for "right and right she'll always be"?

Would it be more like Faye Dunaway's portrayal of Joan Crawford in *Mommie Dearest,* who beats her daughter with wire clothes hangers?

Perhaps you think of the doting stage mother Mama Rose? Or the powerful, shoulder-padded matriarchs of the 1980s family-business dramas *Dynasty, Falcon Crest,* or *Dallas.* Or even the seductive Mrs. Robinson in *The Graduate.*

Hera. Eve. Sarah. Oedipus's mother, Jocasta. Jesus' mother, Mary. The Old Lady in the Shoe. Lady MacBeth. June Cleaver. Reba. From the most ancient stories to the most recent sit-coms; from plays written by Greek dramatists to the works of the modern filmmakers, we have been exposed to a wide variety of mothers. If art imitates life, we can be sure that there is no single, all-encompassing portrait of "Mother." Mothers can be protective, overprotective, selfless, generous, zealous, and jealous. They can advocate, nurture, take, give, suffer, and ignore. Many times one woman encompasses all these characteristics at different times.

As we consider how mothers are portrayed in *The Secret Life of Bees,* we'll need to expand our ideas of *mother* beyond one who gives physical birth. For while the novel is populated by many caring, life-giving, protective, nurturing women, we catch only peripheral glimpses of actual biological mothers. In fact in some ways the novel revolves around the *absence* of Lily's mother, Deborah Fontanel Owens.

The Bible holds up the concept of motherhood beyond biological ties. In Jeremiah, "Rachel is weeping for her children; / she refuses to be comforted for her children, / because they are no more" (Jer. 31:15). Rachel was the mother of Joseph and Benjamin, whose story is told in Genesis, but here the lament is understood to be for the whole of Israel. Rebekah, another matriarch of the faith, receives a blessing that she "increase to thousands upon thousands" (Gen. 24:60, NIV). In Judges, the judge and prophetess Deborah "arose as a mother in Israel" (Judg. 5:7), although the Bible is silent about biological children. Mary was the biological mother of Jesus and perhaps five or six other children. As Jesus dies on the cross, he looks at the beloved disciple and Mary, and declares they are now mother and son and are to regard each other with the same honor and responsibility as blood relatives (Jn. 19:26–27).

As the novel concludes, with Lily saying good-bye to one chapter of her life and stepping into the next, she suddenly recognizes that the deepest longing of her heart—the yearning for a mother—has been satisfied. In an epiphany moment, she recognizes that she has many mothers.

Mothers in the Bible: M Is for Mosaic

Mothers—biological and otherwise—are plentiful in the Bible, from Eve in the first chapters of Genesis to the cosmic mother in Revelation (chap. 12). Taken together, they provide an interesting mosaic of the biblical mother: protective, loyal, and instructive. On the other hand, they can be jealous, scornful, and boastful about their children.

Mothers of the Old Testament

In the patriarchal societies in which the events of the Old Testament took place, biological motherhood was not only desired but was an essential aspect of being a woman. Having children, in particular sons, secured a woman's status in the household and thus society. In a culture where inheritance rights rarely went in favor of the woman, it was important for a woman to have children to provide for her in her declining years. Perhaps one of the worst things in the world was for a woman to not have children. So important was it for a family to have children that social and legal conventions allowed men to have secondary wives ("concubines") and allowed wives who did not bear children to require their female servants to bear children for them, as was the case with Sarah and Hagar.

Difficulty in conception is a theme that runs throughout the Old Testament. Hannah, the mother of Samuel, is "deeply distressed and [prays] to the LORD, and [weeps] bitterly" over her lack of children. She asks for deliverance from her "misery" (1 Sam. 1:10, 11).

Another woman in similar "misery" is Rachel, the beautiful wife of Jacob. The rivalry between her and her not-so-beautiful sister, Leah, is a good example of the importance of motherhood in ancient Israel. Rachel and Leah, along with servants Bilhah and Zilpah, are the mothers of the twelve tribes of Israel (Gen. 29:16 to 30:24; Gen. 35:16–18). Rachel and Leah are wives to Jacob; Jacob loves the younger Rachel more, but Leah bears him sons easily.

Rachel cries to Jacob, "Give me children, or I shall die!" (Gen. 30:1). When she finally has a son, she says "God has taken away my reproach" (30:23).

Likewise Leah recognizes the importance of bearing sons, and believes—apparently wrongly—that this is the way she can get Jacob to love her. After the birth of her first son, she concludes: "Because the LORD has looked upon my affliction; surely now my husband will love me" (Gen. 29:32). After her third son Leah, still vying with Rachel for Jacob's affection, surmises, "Now this time my husband will be joined to me, because I have borne him three sons" (29:34). And after her sixth: "God has endowed me with a good dowry; now my husband will honor me, because I have borne him six sons" (30:20).

The rivalry between the sisters Leah and Rachel causes them to draw their maids into their son-bearing competition.

They may have learned their behavior from their grandmother-in-law Sarai/Sarah, who had trouble conceiving and cultivated a similar rivalry with her Egyptian maid, Hagar (Gen. 16). When Hagar conceived, she "looked with contempt" on Sarai, who treated her so harshly that Hagar ran away from the household, only to be urged by God to return. Later, after Sarah gave birth to Isaac, she insisted that Abraham cast out Hagar and her and Abraham's son, Ishmael, into the wilderness. Sarah's motivation wasn't purely jealousy or concern over her status as the primary wife. She did not want Isaac to consort with the child of her servant. Half-brothers they might be, but as Isaac's mother, it was up to her to be sure that his inheritance— as well as her status—was preserved.

Sarah's daughter-in-law Rebekah was also concerned about the status of her twin sons, Esau and Jacob, in the household. Esau was technically the firstborn son and as such was entitled to a higher leadership role in the family, as well as a double portion of the inheritance. But "Rebekah loved Jacob" (Gen. 25:28). She schemed with Jacob so that an aging Isaac would bestow his death-bed blessing not on the elder Esau, but on the younger son, Jacob. Such blessings (Gen. 27:27–29) were believed to invoke a power that could determine the destiny of the one who received it.

Biological motherhood helped a woman secure her status in the family and in society, but the Old Testament is also full of women who are nurturing caregivers to children who are not their own through childbirth. Consider all the women who protect Moses (Ex. 1:15—2:10). After Pharaoh declares that all male babies must be killed, two midwives, Shiphrah and Puah, go against his orders to follow God and let the infant boys live. When Moses is born, his mother hides him as long as she can, then puts him in a basket in the river to protect him. Moses' sister watches, and when Pharaoh's daughter finds the baby, the sister Miriam gets her mother to be Moses' nurse, and Pharaoh's daughter becomes his adopted mother.

Another woman in the Bible who establishes nurturing motherlike relationships is Naomi, who is so loved by her daughters-in-law that they prefer to travel with Naomi to her country of Judah after their husbands die, rather than return to their own mothers' homes in Moab. One daughter-in-law does return to her people, but Ruth insists on remaining with Naomi, and they develop a reciprocal relationship of care. Naomi advises Ruth about how to become the wife of another man, Boaz. When Ruth has a son, Naomi becomes his nurse, and Ruth is honored.

> Then the women said to Naomi, "Blessed be the LORD, who has not left you this day without next-of-kin; and may his name be renowned in Israel! He shall be to you a restorer of life and a nourisher of your old age; for your daughter-in-law who loves you, who is more to you than seven sons, has borne him." (Ruth 4:14–15)

Mothers in the New Testament

Likewise mothers and mother figures in the New Testament give us a prismatic view of motherhood. Generally they are protective of their offspring in various ways. In a letter to Timothy, Timothy's mother and grandmother are held up for their gifts of instruction in the ways of faith:

> I am reminded of your sincere faith, a faith that lived first in your grandmother Lois and in your mother Eunice and now, I am sure, lives in you. (2 Tim. 1:5)

In the gospels of Matthew and Mark, we find a mother who cries after Jesus to save her demon-possessed daughter (Mt. 15:22–28; Mk. 7:24–30). The story of the Canaanite/Syrophoenician woman has been the source of a number of interpretations. Jesus initially refuses to help this Gentile mother, saying he came to save the Jews. But she is persistent and humbles herself. Jesus commends her faith, and the little girl is healed. The story is notable in two respects: Jesus' reluctance to help the little girl seems harsh, and the mother appears to out-argue Jesus. The mother's success in convincing Jesus is perhaps a unique example of somebody outdebating Jesus about the love of God. Jesus, after all, was the master debater, continually confounding experts in religious law, and brilliantly conveying God's grace in the context of questions that seemed impossible to answer. The motivation behind Jesus' surprising reaction—initially not to heal the girl—in this story has been scrutinized, explained away, defended, and criticized. But the woman's behavior has not been questioned. She is fighting for her little girl. Where the Bible has not given her a name, tradition has: Justa, which means "justice."

Jesus himself imagined motherhood as a role of protection. In his lament over Jerusalem (Mt. 23:37–39; Lk. 13:34–35), he uses motherly language to describe his pity for the city's inhabitants: "How often have I desired to gather your children together as a hen gathers her brood under her wings."

Matthew's gospel also contains a "stage mother" who wants to promote her children at the expense of others (Mt. 20:20–21). The mother of James and John kneels before Jesus asking that when Jesus comes into his kingdom, her sons sit to his right and left.

The New Testament also lifts up a mother who, in addition to being a biological mother, acts as a mother figure to a cousin. Luke's gospel tells us that when Mary discovers her pregnancy, she turns not to her own mother, but to her cousin Elizabeth. Like many of the mothers in the Old Testament, Elizabeth had no children until late in life. Much older than her young cousin, Elizabeth greets Mary with joy and takes her into her home for three months, until the time Elizabeth is to give birth to John the Baptist.

Mothers in *The Secret Life of Bees:* M Is for Missing

If you grew up in a household with a mother—your birth mother, a grandmother, a stepmother—can you imagine what your growing up would have been like without her presence?

A mother fills many roles in the family. She is the boss and the servant. She might be the cook, the janitor, the cheerleader, the source of religion, and the disciplinarian. She might be the one who nurtures, who heals, who provides moral instruction, who encourages education. If there is no father in the household, her role could encompass those functions often ascribed to fathers: the fixer, the breadwinner, the coach.

Much of *The Secret Life of Bees* revolves around the absence of Lily's mother. Lily is haunted by the only memory she has of Deborah—the day Deborah died. Even though Lily's memories of her mother are few and sketchy, Lily longs for a mother and has definite ideas about what a mother should be, namely, *present*. The haunting memory and the secret longing for a mother keep Lily awake. The angry words of her father about her mother are Lily's motivation for leaving home, and a small physical remnant of her mother drives her to Tiburon, South Carolina. Even after she finds welcome in the home of the calendar sisters, the longing does not subside:

> The worst thing was lying there wanting my mother. That's how it had always been; my longing for her nearly always came late at night when my guard was down. I tossed on the sheets, wishing I could crawl into bed with her and smell her skin. I wondered: Had she worn thin nylon gowns to bed? Did she bobby-pin her hair? I could just see her, propped in bed. My mouth twisted as I pictured myself climbing in beside her and putting my head against her breast. I would put it right over hear beating heart and listen. Mama, I would say. And she would look down at me and say, Baby, I'm right here. (*Bees,* 98f.)

By the end of the novel, as Lily reconciles in her heart with her biological mother, she realizes that she has many "mothers." Just as bees in a hive have their specific functions, the women in *The Secret Life of Bees* fill a variety of roles in the household and in Lily's life. Two main mother figures are August and Rosaleen, who are a study in contrasts. Lily compares each of them to the statue of the virgin Mary in the parlor:

> It was plain that Rosaleen had fire in her, too. Not hearth fire, like August, but fire that burns the house down, if necessary, to clean up the mess inside it. Rosaleen reminded me of the statue of Our Lady in the parlor, and I thought, If August is the red heart on Mary's chest, Rosaleen is the fist. (*Bees,* 182)

Lily finds herself in a world populated by surrogate mothers. First is Rosaleen, a "stand-in" mother since the death of Deborah. Lily even fantasizes about having Rosaleen as a mother. Unlike the "Divine Mother" of chapter 1, Rosaleen is a very Earthly mother, a woman who is physically right in the mix with Lily. She resides not only in Lily's heart, but outside Lily, in the flesh.

A woman whose wisdom is enfolded in sarcasm and bald honesty, Rosaleen is one to act without apology or explanation. She has deep affection for Lily and for May, but she is the one who is mostly likely to call it like it is and force an issue. She protects Lily during her time with T. Ray; she comforts Lily during their escape and as Lily struggles to come to grips with her mother's absence. As a mother is both servant and boss to her children, Rosaleen absorbs the presumptions and patronizing ways of Lily even as she cares for Lily. That is, until Rosaleen finds out the real reason for their escape, chiding Lily for her lack of a plan:

> "coming in there saying we're gonna do this and we're gonna do that, and I'm supposed to follow you like a pet dog. You act like you're my keeper. Like I'm some dumb nigger you gonna save." Her eyes were hard and narrow. (*Bees,* 53)

The following morning, Lily finds Rosaleen in a creek, the tempting picture of the mother Lily so strongly desires:

Water beaded across her shoulders, shining like drops of milk, and her breasts swayed in the currents. It wasn't the kind of vision you never really get over. I couldn't help it, I wanted to go and lick the milk beads from her shoulders.

I opened my mouth. I wanted something. Something, I didn't know what. *Mother, forgive.* That's all I could fee. That old longing spread under me like a great lap, holding me tight. (*Bees,* 55)

Mothers in Society: M Is for the Many Works of Justice

Two women in different decades are credited for the inception of Mother's Day. Anna Jarvis wrote letters to Congress to honor the work of her mother, Anna Reeves Jarvis. During the Civil War, Anna Reeves Jarvis had called on mothers—both Northern and Southern—to help the poor, tend the wounded, and work for peace. Julia Ward Howe, who wrote the "Battle Hymn of the Republic," changed her militant stance once she saw the effects of war, and became a tireless worker for peace and women's voting rights. She too called on the women of the world, mothers in particular, to take up the banner of peace.

It might be surprising that Mother's Day started not as a sentimental celebration of one's own mother, but as a recognition that wars and social injustices are painful to all mothers. Likewise Rosaleen's scope expands beyond herself and her charge. She becomes a symbol of the civil rights cause. She is not only a victim of racism, but an instrument of resistance as well. According to Delores S. Williams, black women have been instruments of resistance since Africans were first brought to American shores as slaves. They petitioned for their own freedom, participated in slave revolts, and tried to murder their masters. One slave mother reportedly passed this advice on to her daughter: "Fight, and if you can't fight, kick:

if you can't kick, then bite." And while men were seen as leaders in the civil rights movement, at least as many women participated in demonstrations and organizational meetings.

It is ironic that while Rosaleen protects Lily in the home, she can provide no such protection in public. In fact Lily has to protect Rosaleen in public to a certain degree. Even though she is just a teenager, Lily carries more status in 1964 South Carolina than the middle-aged Rosaleen. If it seems patronizing that Lily speaks for both of them in public, we must remember that Rosaleen carries almost no cultural currency and therefore is not allowed a voice in society.

But Rosaleen does speak out. While Lily understands and goes along with the racist system for safety's sake, Rosaleen resists. In almost every encounter with an authority figure— T. Ray, Brother Gerald, the men at the gas station, Mr. Gaston— Rosaleen resists. She does this in a world in which nothing affords her protection. Even the police and the local minister are complicit in the racist system. And while Rosaleen's registering to vote is a legal act, it goes against the social mores of the South in 1964.

Prejudice goes both ways in *The Secret Life of Bees.* Lily is startled to discover that she can be rejected because of her skin color:

> This was a great revelation—not that I was white but that it seemed like June might not want me here because of my skin color. I hadn't known this was possible—to reject people for being white. (*Bees,* 87)

As Lily falls in love with Zach, she has to come to grips with their racial differences. Lily's solution: God should have made people without skin pigment so that everyone would all be the same.

In addressing the issue of racial difference, some have said that people should be able to look at one another and not notice skin color. Others have said that we should notice the difference in skin color, but that it shouldn't make any difference. While some people maintain a position of "we are all the same inside," others argue the point. They answer that in light of the racist history of America, differences in ethnicity—between Europeans, Latinos, Asians, Native Americans, and African Americans—have resulted in different experiences in education, employment, and lifestyle. God may treasure each one of God's children, and we may all be valued in the eyes of God, but we are all different. Differences in skin color and culture are to be acknowledged and, finally, celebrated.

In *The Secret Life of Bees,* Lily wants to change the situation—erasing or changing skin color. But Zach wants to change people's hearts.

> "We can't think of changing our skin," he said. "Change the world—that's how we gotta think." (*Bees,* 216)

Rosaleen as Mammy?

When T. Ray "pulled [Rosaleen] out of the peach orchard, where she'd worked as one of his pickers," Rosaleen stepped into a role that has been both honored and despised: a black surrogate mother for a white child. The ambivalence about this situation is particularly keen in the South, which held onto the "mammy" tradition long after the Civil War.

If you've seen the film *Gone with the Wind,* you might remember Scarlett O'Hara's Mammy, with all her practical wisdom, bluster, and compassion. It's worthwhile to think about whether it's appropriate to compare Rosaleen and Mammy.

The film depiction was, of course, idealized. The life of a real "mammy" was far more complicated and riddled with sadness, disappointment, hard work, and little reward. At the end of her years, sometimes after raising generations of white children, a trusted and loyal mammy could be turned out to survive—or perish—on her own.

A mammy was a house slave, and her primary duty was to look after the white children of the family. According to

Delores S. Williams, she was the center of a household and controlled its management. She was highly skilled at most or all the domestic tasks, and even business matters. She was often the moral guide of her white charges. Because she was so valuable to the household, she held a relatively large degree of power, authority, and influence in a world in which her fellow slaves had none at all.

Because the white household demanded such devotion from the mammy, we must wonder, What about her own children? What about her own household? Mammies were often forced to put the interests of the white surrogate children above the interests of their own children, who might be sold to other plantations. While a mammy preserved the integrity of the white household, she was unable to encourage the integrity of black families, which were routinely and intentionally separated and dispersed by the institution of slavery. With her authority and influence, however, a mammy was sometimes in a position to stand up for her fellow slaves, and even help in the cause of abolition and escape.

The world of the antebellum mammy is, of course, a far cry from Rosaleen's world. Her surrogate motherhood is not coerced, strictly speaking; she is a paid employee. Also, she has no children or family of her own who suffer neglect because she looks after Lily. It is interesting to note that while T. Ray finds it perfectly suitable to hire a black woman to be the sole source of guidance and care for his daughter, he and a number of other characters find it appalling that the same girl would live in a community of black mother figures.

Mother: M Is for the Many Facets of Her

Just as the song M-O-T-H-E-R idealizes the lyricist's mother, and just as *Gone with the Wind* idealizes the role of Mammy, it is easy to consider *mother,* whether biological or surrogate, in stereotypical terms. In an ideal world, our mothers do take care of us, love us, sacrifice for us, protect us, tell us we are great. The two primary surrogate mothers in *The Secret Life of Bees* fit into this world, with their common sense and profound wisdom, their unfailing and loving encouragement of Lily, and their devotion to community.

If there are any shadows lurking in August's and Rosaleen's psyches, we are unaware of them. They have personalities, to be sure. They have their share of challenges and sorrows in their families and in the broader society. But these mostly serve to give them wisdom, courage, and determination. We readers aren't privy to internal struggles or temptations, or characteristics we might see as flaws. The bold action by Rosaleen in the opening chapter that leads to her brutal beating and imprisonment is treated almost comically; we readers aren't given many clues about her motivation for such action.

The Bible, on the other hand, gives us several mothers who were caught in dilemmas. As we have seen, many were trapped between their biological limitations, their own desires and insecurities, and the expectations and laws of society.

We must take care against adopting impossible ideals for motherhood. Consider the mother whose daughter would die if she could not find a suitable donor for a bone marrow transplant. After all other family members had tested negative, the mother and her husband conceived another child in hopes of providing a suitable donor for the older child. Was the mother a compassionate protector of her beloved daughter? Or did she ruthlessly plot to put the life of another child at risk in order to protect her firstborn?

Even the Mother of the Year carries shadows. Even the most perfect mother imaginable harbors her secret guilt. The mother who sacrifices her own education to stay at home and care for her children may find herself holding resentment. The mother who weeps when her children go off to kindergarten or college may be secretly relieved that she can have the house to herself. To deny those feelings is to deny that God created all women as full human beings with the right to claim the full range of human emotions, even those not captured in our idealized picture of motherhood.

QUESTIONS FOR DISCUSSION

1. What do you think of when you think of the term *mother?* Is your concept of motherhood based on your own experience of being mothered?

2. What would your life growing up have been like without a mother? Or what was growing up without a mother like, if your mother was not present during your childhood? If you are a mother, what would your life be like without children?

3. What are the points of contact between the mothers in the Bible and the "mothers" of the novel? Do you find any sharp points of disconnect?

4. Do you think Lily is right that pigment should be erased so that we are all one color?

5. Does Lily idealize her mother? Does she idealize the *idea* of motherhood?

FURTHER READING

Tikva Frymer-Kinsky, *Reading the Women of the Bible*. New York: Random House, 2002.

Anne Lamott, *Operating Instructions: A Journal of My Son's First Year*. New York: Pantheon, 1993.

Stephanie Paulsell, *Honoring the Body*. San Francisco: Jossey-Bass, 2003.

Delores S. Williams, *Sisters in the Wilderness*. Maryknoll, N.Y.: Orbis Books, 1993.

CHAPTER 3

Sister
MAY'S RITUAL

*And pointing to his disciples, he said, "Here are my mother
and my brothers! For whoever does the will of my Father
in heaven is my brother and sister and mother."*

(Mt. 12:49–50)

*But here, now, surrounded by stinging bees on all sides and
the motherless place throbbing away, I knew that these bees
were not a plague at all. It felt like the queen's attendants
were out here in a frenzy of love, caressing me in a
thousand places. Look who's here, it's Lily. She is so weary
and lost. Come on, bee sisters. I was the stamen in the
middle of a twirling flower. The center of all their
comforting.*

(*Bees*, 151)

Just as *The Secret Life of Bees* hums with the constant presence of mother figures, the novel also pulses with the idea of sisterhood. While Kidd's book has a decided lack of biological mothers, you will find plenty of sisters, particularly the "calendar sisters."

Each of the sisters has a distinct personality and a different role within the Boatwright family. August, the eldest, runs the beekeeping operation. She is often the voice of wisdom. She organizes the worship life of the Daughters of Mary. June can be moody and hard-hearted. She teaches school and provides music for the worship services. May, the tender-spirited sister whom Lily describes as simpleminded, runs the kitchen. All single women, the sisters create a caring household in which each of their gifts is employed, each of their needs is met, and each is allowed to express herself fully.

This is true especially for May. After losing her twin sister, May needs special care. The other two sisters oblige. They accommodate her personality, tiptoeing around subjects of woe that may cause her distress. They also help her cope, giving her soothing baths and supplying the idea of the wailing wall.

Sisters in the Bible

The Bible, particularly the Old Testament, is the story of families. The people who wrote the Bible and recorded the history of the ancient Hebrew people didn't just tell about the main actors in history. Genealogy was important to the Hebrew people, and so we know about their extended families as well: mothers, daughters, brothers, fathers. We begin with the first family: Adam and Eve, followed by their sons Cain and Abel, then Seth. Then come daughters, and then the second generation of sons and daughters. Not only is Noah saved in the ark, but also his entire family. The patriarch and matriarch of Israel—Abraham and Sarah—appear with their entire lineage. Moses is born into a family, adopted into another family, and married into another family. And the story of David is nothing if not an extended family saga.

Because we have so many families in the Old Testament, we can find a lot of sisters in the Bible. Many times, however, we read of sisters in the context of their brothers rather than in relation to one another. In fact, a number of prominent sisters in the Bible appear to be the *only* daughters in their families. Miriam, for example, is sister to Moses and Aaron. Dinah, Leah's daughter, is the only sister named among the siblings for whom the twelve tribes of Israel are named. And Tamar is the only daughter of King David listed in 1 Chronicles 3:9.

Sisters in the Old Testament

In families today, brothers, especially big brothers, often assume the role of protecting their sisters. They may protect them from the schoolyard bully, and they may scrutinize and screen potential boyfriends or husbands.

But in the Old Testament family stories, having a brother, even a number of brothers, does not necessarily afford a girl protection. For example, in Genesis 34, we have the tragic story of Dinah, Jacob's daughter by Leah. Dinah is "humbled" or "dishonored" when Shechem, a prince and son of Hamor, the chief of the land, "lay with her." According to the Bible, Shechem falls in love with Dinah and wants to marry her. He even gets Hamor to try to arrange the marriage and establish peaceful relations between the two families.

If Dinah wanted to marry Shechem (the Bible never tells us what she thinks), this would be a good arrangement for her. Brides were expected to be virgins, and Dinah is no longer a virgin. It might be difficult to find another husband. Dinah's brothers are so outraged by the sexual encounter, however, that they trick Hamor into having all the men of his city circumcised. While those men are recovering, the brothers kill them and sack the city. Some scholars say the Bible is not clear on whether the encounter was a rape, or whether Dinah was a willing partner, though the NRSV says Shechem "seized her and lay with her by force" (Gen. 34:2).

Did Dinah want to marry Shechem? We never know because the story centers not around her, but around the brothers' bloodthirsty revenge.

Another tragic "sister" story is that of Tamar, full sister to Absalom and half-sister to Amnon—all offspring of King David (2 Sam. 13). After Amnon tricks Tamar and "forces" her—we can definitely read this as rape—her brother Absalom wants revenge. He tells Tamar to keep quiet about the rape, and then plots a bloody revenge against his half-brother. Amnon's murder leads to the battle between Absalom and King David.

While brothers in the Old Testament are quick to seek revenge over the abuse of their sisters, the sisters themselves never get much of a voice in expressing their wishes. Just as motherhood was prized in ancient Israel, virgin status was also crucial for a woman until she was married. As Dinah's brothers say of her non-virgin state, "should he treat our sister as a harlot?" We don't know what happened to Dinah. Tamar lived with Absalom as "a desolate woman."

Are sister-to-sister relations in the Old Testament any better? In chapter 2 we looked at two sisters, Leah and Rachel, and their jealous rivalry. We don't know much about the relationships between other sisters, such as the seven daughters of the Midian priest, one of whom—Zipporah—married Moses (Ex. 2:16–22).

We do have at least two examples of sisters who worked together to achieve a goal. The daughters of Lot conspired to get their father drunk and sleep with him so that through them his lineage would be preserved (Gen. 19:30–36). In Numbers, we learn of the five daughters of Zelophehad: Mahlah, Noah, Hoglah, Milcah, and Tirzah. In chapter 26, God instructs Moses how to divide the land for inheritance. In chapter 27, the sisters approach Moses and argue that since their father died without siring a son, they should have a right to claim an inheritance. God agrees with the sisters and declares that if a family has no son, the daughters receive the inheritance.

If they want to keep it, however, they must marry within the tribe.

Sisters in the New Testament

In the New Testament we get two stories about two sisters: Mary and Martha of Bethany. Perhaps the more well-known of the two stories is in Luke's gospel (Lk. 10:38–42). In this story, Martha has received Jesus into her house and is scurrying about with "many tasks." We can imagine that she has many guests besides Jesus. While Martha serves, Mary sits at Jesus' feet to hear his teaching. Martha asks Jesus to tell Mary to get off her duff and help, but Jesus says that Mary is doing what she should.

This story sets the sisters up in competition, or at least in contrast. It can be interpreted that one sister made the right choice and the other the wrong choice. Martha scurries about trying to be the gracious hostess, performing superfluous tasks, and carrying unnecessary anxiety that things be just so. Sometimes she is almost seen as shrewish, complaining that her sister Mary should likewise be just as anxious.

This is just one interpretation. We must remember that the house belongs to Martha, and she must be hospitable to her guests: codes and rules of hospitality are highly important in her culture and must be followed. Martha cannot be faulted for supplying her guests with food and drink. Jesus does say that Mary has chosen well in choosing to listen to his teaching, but his comments to Martha could be an indicator that the meal and service might be simplified. Perhaps she doesn't need to serve such a fancy, elaborate meal.

John's gospel also tells the story of the two sisters of Bethany (Jn. 11). In this story, Martha is a beloved friend of Jesus, as is her brother, Lazarus. Lazarus has died, and Jesus comes to Bethany. While Mary stays in the house, Martha meets Jesus on the road. In this story, the sisters aren't compared with each other, but are both viewed as faithful disciples.

Sisters in *The Secret Life of Bees*

The Boatwright household is run by sisters. They have developed a system of care and nurture that involves taking care of physical needs, such as cooking meals and providing income. It also involves taking care of one another's spiritual, psychological, and emotional needs.

Knowing how to care for someone you love can be difficult. In the novel the family must tiptoe around June's views on marriage. On the one hand, they don't want to hurt her feelings; on the other hand, they believe marrying Neil would be a good thing in her life. June and August also have had to learn to navigate May's fragile emotional state by helping her cope with—or avoid—the world's burdens.

Sisters are in unique positions to give mutual care. They share the same parent or parents and often the same formative childhood experiences. If they have shared the experiences of growing up, then they may have the same values, the same worldview. They might not only look alike but also have the same sense of humor, the same interests, the same facial expressions.

On the other hand, each is a unique individual. The uncanny closeness of May and her twin sister, April, had tragic results when April committed suicide. Consider how the death of a sibling is different from the death of a parent or a child or a friend. Besides an emotional tie, siblings share a generational tie. When a sibling dies, one can feel more keenly one's own mortality. And when a twin dies, the effect is multiplied.

> "When April died, something in May died, too. She never was normal after that. It seemed like the world itself became May's twin sister." (*Bees,* 97)

Also, consider that April killed herself at age fifteen, in the midst of the turbulent teen years. That is just a year older than Lily, and we know the issues Lily is facing. She must contend with her budding sexuality and new ventures in forming relationships. She is becoming more and more aware of how the outside world affects her and the people she loves, especially in matters of race and discrimination. Also, the critical issue of her mother's death and absence is coming to a head. She must learn to deal with hurt, anger, and loss on an adult level.

What were you going through when you were fifteen? A teenager discovers where she or he fits into the family and into society. A teenager discovers things he or she is good at or interested in. Remembering our lives at fifteen might help us understand the effect of April's death on May.

> "Our mother said she was like Mary, with her heart on the outside of her chest. Mother was good about taking care of her, but when she died, it fell to me and June. We tried for years to get May some help. She saw doctors, but they didn't have any idea what to do with her except put her away. So June and I came up with this idea of a wailing wall." (*Bees,* 97)

If we are lucky, we have someone who can help us navigate those complicated teenage years. May is especially fortunate in that her two sisters agreed to help her navigate her life far beyond the teen years. In many ways, May is a normal, intelligent woman. She is capable of building deep, significant friendships. She can read and cook. She can contribute to a conversation, have opinions. She feels joy as well as pain.

But her strong reactions to painful situations cripple her ability to lead an entirely normal life. Part of the way her sisters help her is to build routines or accommodate those that May herself develops, such as having the perfect banana. Routines can be comforting and reliable, especially when we are depressed or suffer from tragedy.

The Four Rs: Routines, Rituals, Rites, and Religion

Do you have a morning routine? Can you not talk to anyone without that second cup of coffee—even when it's decaf? Can you not get your day started without a shower? Fall asleep without a bath?

Some things we do in the same manner every time: make coffee in a certain way, clean our desks before we leave work. Perhaps you cannot sit down and write a letter without lighting a candle, or maybe you clean the house to certain music. We are creatures of habit. We buy a particular brand of toothpaste, call mother or do our laundry on a certain day of the week, hum when we are angry or sad. You may lay peonies on your grandmother's grave every Memorial Day. You may spend every Labor Day weekend in the same beach-house.

In the movie *Misery*, James Caan plays an ex-smoking author. After finishing each novel, he carefully strikes a match, holds it to the end of his cigarette, and draws deeply. In the movie *It's a Wonderful Life*, George Bailey makes a wish for a million dollars every time he goes into the local drug store, then cries "Hot dog!" Baseball players are notorious for their good-luck rituals: Wade Boggs ate chicken before every game; manager Sparky Anderson would never step on a foul line as he walked to or from the pitcher's mound.

Church life is full of rituals from the moment we walk in the doors. We may look for someone special, say hello to the same group of people clustered by the coffee carafe. We may sit in the same pew. After church, we may routinely go to a fellowship time. These are our individual rituals. We also perform rituals together, such as say the Lord's Prayer, sing the Gloria Patri, and participate in the Lord's supper. Not only do we do the same things but we do them in the same way and at the same point in the service. As they conclude their service in *The Secret Life of Bees,* The Daughters of Mary ceremoniously touch the fading red heart of the statue of the black Mary.

Rituals, habits, and rites are familiar activities that can bring tremendous comfort. They give us something to do when we don't know what to do. For a new widow whose life has been turned upside down, a simple morning routine provides her with something dependable to follow. Or consider the case of a middle-aged man who prays from the Book of Common Prayer. Over the years, he has ceased reading the prayers, now knowing them by heart. He finds great comfort in the familiarity of the words. He feels at peace, and as he feels at peace, he senses God moving in his heart.

When Lily, Rosaleen, June, and August search for the missing May, they recite the Hail Mary, the same prayer they pray every night with their rosaries. Morning showers, Memorial Day flowers, the Doxology, the Rosary. What is the difference between all these activities? What do they have in common? Which would you call a sacrament? Which would you call a ritual? Which merely a habit? What's the difference?

Let's look at some of the characteristics of ritual:

• It is repetitive.

• It is done in a prescribed manner.

• This prescribed manner is an established one. It isn't made up on the spur of the moment.

• It is done at a specially appointed time.

All these things are true of how churches celebrate the eucharist, or the Lord's supper. However, we could also say this about brushing our teeth.

Religious rituals have another component. Our morning dental hygiene routine probably carries no deeper meaning than keeping our teeth clean. Religious rites, on the other hand, have a meaning that goes beyond the superficial act. In *The Secret Life of Bees,* August explains how worship of the black Mary came into being:

> "And so," August said, "the people cried and danced and clapped their hands. They went one at a time and touched their hands to her chest, wanting to grab on to the solace in her heart.

"They did this every Sunday in the praise house, dancing and touching her chest, and eventually they painted a red heart on her breast so the people would have a heart to touch.

"Our Lady filled their hearts with fearlessness and whispered to them plans of escape. The bold ones fled, finding their way north, and those who didn't lived with a raised fist in their hearts. And if ever it grew weak, they would only have to touch her heart again." (*Bees*, 109–10)

When the Daughters of Mary touch the heart of the black Mary at the close of their worship, they are doing something that generations of African Americans have done, including the first generation of slaves. Note how each person touches the heart in a different way, combining a communal ritual with his or her own special way of observing it.

A religious rite is repetitive and ceremonial, with certain rules about how it is to be conducted (we might imagine a way of touching Mary's heart that would not be appropriate), and it is solemn. But in *The Secret Life of Bees* the act itself of touching the heart conveys a spirit of comfort and strength drawn from a larger, more powerful, divine presence.

Christians have another category of this kind of repetitive, ceremonial activity: sacrament. Sacraments, such as baptism and the Lord's supper, are understood to be means of God's grace. Most definitions of sacrament convey the idea of a "visible means"—something we can see and witness—for an "invisible" or "inward" grace. That is, what God does through the sacrament cannot be observed by the human senses, but works in the heart and soul of a person.

In the example of the Lord's supper, churches have many articulations and understandings of exactly how God expresses God's grace in the bread and wine. Churches pass down many descriptions of exactly how God works *through* or *within* or *by means of* the elements. But what all these have in common is that God is in active relationship with the person who is taking the Lord's supper. The consumption of the bread and wine would have no meaning at all if God were not a part of the picture.

Another important distinction for Christians is how we understand Jesus to be involved in the creation of sacraments. The Catholic Church understands that God acts in the sacraments because Jesus Christ instituted them. Since the Middle Ages, the Catholic Church has observed seven sacraments: baptism, confirmation, eucharist, reconciliation (penance), anointing of the sick, marriage, and holy orders. Other denominations, such as Eastern Orthodox, recognize seven sacraments as well. The Episcopal church elevates baptism and eucharist as the two primary sacraments, with the other five as minor sacraments. Protestants of the reformed tradition, such as Lutherans and Disciples of Christ, generally understand only two rituals to be sacraments, sanctioned explicitly by Jesus Christ: baptism and eucharist.

The More Things Change?

One of the characteristics of ritual is its consistency over a period of time. When we celebrate the Lord's supper and repeat the words of institution, we understand we are saying the same words ("this is my body, this is my blood") that Jesus said.

In *The Secret Life of Bees,* if the meaning behind the heart-touching has remained the same through the generations, the Daughters of Mary are seeking solace in the same manner as the slaves who touched her heart more than a century before. But sometimes meanings or understandings behind rituals change.

Take again the example of the Lord's supper. We understand Jesus gave us this ritual, but let us remember that Jesus was eating a Passover meal, as scholars generally, but not unanimously, agree. He was celebrating a *Jewish* holiday and participating in a *Jewish* ritual. The bread and wine at the meal already had meanings (see Ex. 12). The wine signified the blood that the Hebrew people, still in captivity in Egypt, put across their doorways to save their firstborn when God slew the firstborn of the Egyptians. The bread was unleavened, as the Hebrew people had to flee in such haste that the bread did not have time to rise. At the night of the first Lord's supper, Jesus gave new meanings to the elements. The bread is his body given, or broken, for his disciples. The wine is his blood shed for the forgiveness of sin.

As the Daughters close their celebration of the Feast of Mary, they have a eucharistic moment with the honey cakes. They feed one another bits of bread in turn. But instead of the cake representing the body of Jesus, the Daughters of Mary say, "This is the body of the Blessed Mother" (226). The religion of the Daughters of Mary is indeed a blend of tradition and elements unique to them. They pray the Rosary as Catholics around the world do. But other elements of the service are decidedly nontraditional. August explained their religious practice: "May and June and I take our mother's Catholicism and mix in our own ingredients. I'm not sure what you call it, but it suits us" (90).

Rosaleen also found her own mode of religious expression, when what was offered to her didn't suit her [five hours of church being "enough religion to kill a full-grown person" (29)]. The Baptist church Lily and T. Ray attend seems to do nothing for T. Ray and leaves Lily flat.

Religious services that leave us flat don't encourage our connection with God. They might not even offer a way for us to truly give praise to God. Churches across the country are wrestling with new styles of music, prayer, sermons, even architecture, to try to make a meaningful worship experience for people for whom traditional styles are not working. Some churches no longer refer to God as "Father," understanding that God is neither solely male nor solely female. Many African

American churches use African American images of Jesus rather than older pictures of a white Jesus.

We all want our religious experiences to be meaningful. August's comment that her religion "suits" the sisters raises an interesting point. Although we want our religion to suit us, we need to take care to remember that the main point of worship is not our having a pleasant experience. Although our comfort and inspiration are certainly a benefit of a healthy worship life, we must remember that the central figure in worship is not us, but God. As we ask ourselves what makes for a meaningful worship experience—be it church, small groups, or our own devotional lives—we would do well to ask not only how well we "like" an experience, but how it encourages our connection to God. Christians might also ask how worship deepens their relationship with and understanding of Christ. Of the rituals in *The Secret Life of Bees,* which seem to make a connection to God and which seem mostly to soothe an individual? Which do both? Are there any that seem inappropriate? Why?

Sister, Sister

When we look at the Old Testament and read tragic stories of families, we may feel uncomfortable. Reading the tragedies of Tamar and Dinah, we may think that it is somehow a sister's lot to be submissive to her brothers. If we can't find many good examples of sisterhood, we may think our religion doesn't think woman-to-woman relationships are very important. Or we may think that the Bible simply does not speak to our situations and therefore has nothing to offer us.

But it's helpful to keep in mind what has been said about the Bible, that it is not a *prescription for* life, but a *description of* life. From what we can tell from the Bible, brothers had more power than sisters in ancient family systems. But the New Testament gives us examples of strong women who ran households, such as Martha. And the overriding message in the letters of Paul and in the words and actions of Jesus is that all are equal and valuable in the eyes of God, equipped with gifts and graces.

Also, some biblical stories are very spare in providing us information, and some of that information can be ambiguous. Often it takes an extensive knowledge of ancient cultures to flesh out the stories the Bible gives us. Or we must learn to sift through biblical clues to figure out the point the writer was trying to make. Sometimes every single word is important.

Unlike the Bible, novels often give us a lot more description and be far more explicit in making their points. In *The Secret Life of Bees,* each of the sisters has gifts and graces, and the household allows each of them to express them. In fact, we can imagine that these gifts—as well as each sister's shortcomings—determine how the household runs. August seems to have special, almost mystical, insight into the human heart, and so she organizes the religious services. June's beloved cello playing fits in nicely with the religious services and can express the mood of the household at other times: sorrow, anger, joy, humor. May loves to cook, and so she cooks for the family. Besides filling functions, the sisters provide for one another a household of love. Each, in her own way, is powerful and fulfilled.

Likewise, *The Secret Life of Bees* gives us a picture of alternative modes of religious expression in situations where accepted practices fail to provide acceptable, fulfilling worship experiences. Such illustrations may lead us into a rich exploration of our own worship life and encourage us to try new and creative ways of worshiping God and connecting with our Creator. But we must take care. If our standard is based solely on what "feels good" to us, we miss the point of spirituality. Also, even if, like the women in *The Secret Life of Bees,* we find our current religious practices outdated, meaningless, even oppressive or offensive, we must take care not to throw the baby out with the bathwater. The Bible and church tradition—either our own tradition or the tradition of another denomination—are rich sources of inspiration in strengthening our relationship with God.

QUESTIONS FOR DISCUSSION

1. Can people who are not related by blood be as much a "sister" or "brother" to you as one with whom you share at least one parent?

2. Why is everyone so reluctant to give June advice about marrying Neil?

3. Many literary characters are called "Christ figures"—Benjy in Faulkner's *The Sound and the Fury* or Andy in *The Shawshank Redemption,* for example. In these cases, critics believe the author wants the readers to understand the character has some characteristics of Jesus, such as his suffering, his dying, his divinity, his wisdom. In *The Secret Life of Bees,* August compares May to Mary. Do you agree with the comparison? What are the advantages and disadvantages of making such comparisons between characters and people such as Mary and Jesus?

4. When is it appropriate to change religious practices? How can we know when our religious practices connect us to God, and when they mostly make us feel good?

FURTHER READING

Carole Saline, *Sisters,* ed. Melissa Stein, with photographs by Sharon Wohlmuth. Philadelphia: Running Press, 1994.

Keith Watkins, *The Great Thanksgiving.* St. Louis: Chalice Press, 1995.

Barbara Brown Taylor, *The Preaching Life.* Cambridge, Mass.: Cowley Publications, 1993.

Satoko Yamaguchi. *Mary and Martha.* Maryknoll, N.Y.: Orbis, 2002.

CHAPTER 4

Daughter
LILY'S REBIRTH

*Do you not know that all of us who have been baptized
into Christ Jesus were baptized into his death? Therefore
we have been buried with him by baptism into death, so
that just as Christ was raised from the dead by the glory of
the Father, so we too might walk in newness of life.*

(Rom. 6:3–4)

*Leaning back on my elbows, I slid down till the water
sealed over my head. I held my breath and listened to the
scratch of river against my ears, sinking as far as I could
into that shimmering, dark world.*

(Bees, 56)

*I thought about [Mother Nature] the next morning when I
woke beside the creek in a bed of kudzu vines....Day one
of my new life, I said to myself. That's what this is.*

(Bees, 57)

At the beginning of *The Secret Life of Bees,* Lily describes how she hears bees in the walls of her bedroom during the day and how at night she watches them fly about her room. "I want to say they showed up like the angel Gabriel appearing to the Virgin Mary" (2).

Indeed, bees are divine emissaries as they hum in and out of the novel. Their constant presence provides comfort, yet it prods Lily to move beyond her current circumstance and embrace something new: a new life, a new attitude, a new outlook, a new sense of wonder. The bees beckon Lily to leave the house she shares with her father, and they welcome her to her new home with the Boatwright sisters. The bees surround Lily as she grapples with issues of loss and longing. They accompany May's body to the cemetery; they mourn along with the calendar sisters. One of Lily's surrogate mothers tells her that bees signal death, the other that bees symbolize resurrection.

In chapter 3, we looked at religious rituals and sacraments and how they can connect us with God. Many people understand that in addition to formal sacraments such as baptism and the Lord's supper, we can experience God's presence in all that surrounds us. Everyday acts such as feeding a child or setting a table for a dinner party for dear friends can become sacramental—a vehicle for God's grace—if we understand that we are touching the holy in what we do. Many poets have described the workings of God in nature's rhythms, the face of God in a loved one, or the presence of God in rocks, trees, or flocks of birds. August's grandmother could hear bees sing the Christmas story: "You can hear silent things on the other side of the everyday world that nobody else can. Big Mama had those kind of ears" (144).

Many people also report that God has unexpectedly punched through the fabric of their lives to guide them in new directions, without their even asking God or praying, and sometimes against their will. A popular movie sparks revelation in the heart of a flight attendant and deepens her understanding of Jesus' life and death. A lengthy hospital stay causes a middle-aged mother with a new hip to stop feeling sorry for herself when she witnesses people worse off than she is. A chance conversation with a stranger in a remote national park parking lot clarifies a complex life issue for a young hiker. The flight attendant, the mother, and the hiker each ascribes the experience to God's coming unbidden into their lives.

In *The Secret Life of Bees,* something mysterious and divine, yet strong and unmistakable, pulls Lily from her difficult, if not abusive, life with her widowed father:

> You could say I'd never had a true religious moment, the kind where you know yourself spoken to by a voice that seems other than yourself, spoken to so genuinely you see the words shining on trees and clouds. But I had such a moment right then, standing in my own ordinary room. I heard a voice say, *Lily Melissa Owens, your jar is open.* (*Bees,* 41)

Later, as Lily looks for a sign from God, she comes upon that dearly familiar icon of the black Mary on a jar of honey in the general store. "I realized it for the first time in my life: there is nothing but mystery in the world, how it hides behind the fabric of our poor, browbeat days, shining brightly, and we don't even know it" (63).

Daughters in the Bible

As we look at people in terms of the roles they play in families and society, we examine them as they are in their relationships. A father isn't just a father; he's *somebody's* father. An aunt is an aunt to a niece or a nephew. We look at May as a sister by looking also at those to whom she is a sister.

Lily, however, has to take on her role as daughter without having the benefit of a parent who is present both physically and emotionally. How can she best be a daughter to a mother who died when she was four? How can she be a daughter to a father whose love and concern for her are questionable?

Just as *mother* in the Bible can mean more than a biological mother, *daughter* can imply more than a biological daughter. *Daughters* can imply a people, identified by race or region, such as "daughters of Zion." Jesus identifies one of the women he heals as a "daughter of Abraham" (Lk 13:16). In Psalm 144, the psalmist, praying for deliverance from enemies and a prosperous future, asks God, "May our sons in their youth be like plants full grown, our daughters like corner pillars cut for the building of a palace" (Ps. 144:12).

Daughters in the Old Testament

As we think about the patriarchal societies of the ancient world, we should recognize how vulnerable daughters could be. Community leaders could decide to give not just their own daughters in marriage but also the daughters of the whole tribe in marriage to men of another tribe. These intertribal marriages could signify peace, political alliance, and mutual interest. A lot was at stake in having daughters who were suitable to be given in such marriage. Women's behavior was important. The prophet Isaiah relates the humiliation of the "daughters of Zion" caused by their flashy dressing and haughty, wanton behavior (Isa. 3:16–26).

One of the most tragic daughter stories in the Old Testament is that of Jephthah's daughter (see Judg. 11). We know more about Jephthah than we do his daughter, whose name we are never told. Jephthah the Gileadite was a warrior who became chief of Gilead. In a war vow before his battle with the Ammonites, he promises God that if he is victorious, he will sacrifice whoever comes from his house to greet him. The one who greets him is his daughter, his only child. Jephthah is devastated and subtly tries to blame the tragedy on the girl: "Alas, my daughter! You have brought me very low; you have become the cause of great trouble to me. For I have opened my mouth to the LORD, and I cannot take back my vow" (Judg. 11:35b).

The girl puts the issue back where it belongs. Note how many times in the following verse she uses the words *you* or *your:* "My father, if you have opened your mouth to the LORD, do to me according to what has gone out of your mouth, now that the LORD has given you vengeance against your enemies" (v. 36). The girl further assumes agency in the tragedy, asking that she be given two months to mourn. After her sacrifice, the "daughters of Israel" hold a special yearly remembrance in her honor.

The tragedy of Jephthah's daughter—often compared with the story of Abraham and Isaac (Gen. 22)—can be seen as an injunction against child sacrifice as it was practiced in the ancient world. Archaeological evidence points to such sacrifice in times of hardship, such as war or famine.

In the broader context of Israel's history, the story of Jephthah's daughter also can be seen as a statement about what happens to the most vulnerable members of society when a society deteriorates. Look especially at Judges 19—21. Another daughter, known only as a concubine (or secondary wife), becomes angry at her husband and runs home to her father. In a gruesome and tragic tale, neither man affords the daughter any protection. The father does not protect her from her husband; the husband, to protect his own safety, turns her out into a mob of men bent on violence. Her rape, death, and mutilation set in motion a downward spiral of slaughter that concludes with the abduction of virgins from two tribes, including "daughters of Shiloh," who are forced to become wives for the tribe of Benjamin.

The close of the book of Judges is brutal. Yet it is followed by the book of Ruth, also set in the times of the judges. We discussed this sweet mother-daughter story of mutual care in chapter 2. Here, a Hebrew mother who loses her husband and two sons, implores her daughters-in-law to return to their own mothers. Ruth persists and becomes "more to (Naomi) than seven sons" (Ruth 4:15). Each woman helps ensure a secure future for the other.

Daughters in the New Testament

The New Testament also gives us stories of daughters. In chapter 2 we discussed the daughter of the Syrophoenecian (or Canaanite) woman whom Jesus heals. Jesus also heals the daughter of a ruler named Jairus (Mt. 9:18–25; Mk. 5:22–43; Lk. 8:41–56). The healing story is really the healing of two daughters, however. In each of the accounts Jairus, a leader of the synagogue, comes to Jesus concerned about his daughter. In Mark and in Luke, she is ill; in Matthew, she has already died. In each account, Jesus is interrupted by the touch of a woman who has been bleeding vaginally for twelve years. The nature of her condition would have rendered her ritually unclean and, therefore, excluded from society for more than a decade. Jesus calls this woman "daughter," telling her that her faith has made her well and that she can go away in full health. He then proceeds to Jairus's home. By this time in Mark and Luke the girl has died. But Jesus heals her, then orders that she be fed.

When we read the Bible, we must read carefully for clues from the author. Every word may be significant. The story of Jairus's daughter in Mark and Luke tells us that the little girl is twelve years old. That is, she is on the cusp of the age of marriage in that culture. Interestingly, in all three accounts, the woman who is healed has had a hemorrhage, or has been bleeding from the vagina, for twelve years. We readers are supposed to make a connection between these two "daughters." What connections do you see?

Freedom and Forgiveness: Daughters in *The Secret Life of Bees*

Each woman in the Bible is the daughter of someone, whether or not she is mentioned specifically as a daughter.

Likewise, each woman in *The Secret Life of Bees* is a daughter. Rosaleen, whom we know primarily as one of Lily's two surrogate mothers, remembers and honors her own mother. She keeps and often beholds a photograph of her mother. She talks admiringly about how her mother labored long and hard to support her seven children. Rosaleen might not keep in touch with her siblings, but she remembers her hardworking mother.

Lily's other surrogate mother, August, also fondly remembers her mother and the household of love she created for her four daughters. Lily recognizes the longing in August's heart for her mother: "August set down the jar she was working on, and there was a mix of sorrow and amusement and longing across her face, and I thought, *She is missing her mother*" (143). Lily has no such luxury of fond remembrances and must navigate the role of daughter with only a few items her mother left: a pair of gloves, a photograph, a mysterious icon of Mary, and a remembered smell of cold cream.

Lily and Freedom

As a girl becomes a woman, she naturally tries to establish herself as independent of her mother. Girls try new fashions, new words, new dances. She may test the boundaries of what is acceptable. She may want to start spending time alone with boys. She may want to explore new career options. She may develop her own opinions about politics and world events. She may challenge her parents' basic understandings of right and wrong. As a girl comes into her own, she can perceive even the best mother as a constraint to her freedom. A girl can feel trapped by everything from her mother's taste in clothing to her moral code.

Without her biological mother, Lily undergoes a different struggle for freedom. Having escaped the "jar" of her home in Sylvan and the immediate threat of her father's wrath, Lily continues to be held captive by the longing for her mother—curiosity about her life and guilt associated with her death. In chapter 2, we discussed Lily's deep longing for a mother. It plagues her and catches her off guard. When Lily and August check the beehives one day, the bees begin to alight on Lily, covering her body. Lily undergoes a mystical, euphoric experience in a field of clover:

> Then, without warning, all the immunity wore off, and I felt the hollow, spooned-out space between my navel and breastbone begin to ache. The motherless place. I could see my mother in the closet, the stuck window, the suitcase on the floor. I heard the shouting, then the explosion. I almost doubled over. I lowered my arms, but I didn't open my eyes. How could I live the whole rest of my life knowing these things? (*Bees*, 150–51)

Lily does not long for just a mother: she longs for a home and a normal family life. Rosaleen warns Lily about getting too attached to the calendar sisters, particularly when their stay at the Boatwright household is premised on a lie. But Lily pleads with Rosaleen not to share their secret. Rosaleen accuses Lily of living in a "dream world," but Lily wants to keep her secret in order to stay and lead a "regular life."

Lily becomes trapped in a quandary. While she wants to preserve her "dream world," she also wants desperately to come clean with August, whom she has grown to love. Especially after Lily discovers that her mother had stayed at the Boatwright house, Lily yearns to talk with August about her mother and reveal the real reason she and Rosaleen came to Tiburon. But time and time again, her fears prevent the conversation.

Lily also longs for Zach. She harbors normal pubescent sexual desires for him, in addition to feelings of friendship. But the longing is compounded by the seeming impossibility of a relationship between a white girl and a black boy in 1964 South Carolina. Tied in with her feelings of longing is the strong determination not to settle down with anyone. Lily clings to possibility and to the freedom associated with it.

Captivity and liberation is a major theme in *The Secret Life of Bees*. The black Mary, "Our Lady of Chains," was a symbol of liberation to captive slaves. The highlight of Mary Day is a reenactment of her captivity and release. Rosaleen repeatedly struggles with physical captivity: she is restrained while men beat her; she is held in jail; she is even tied down in the hospital. Zach, too, is a character of captivity and liberation. Like Rosaleen, he is put in jail. But his bigger struggle is to break free of societal mores and become an attorney.

Lily and Forgiveness

As the mystery of Deborah Fontanel Owens unfolds, Lily's feelings surrounding her mother undergo a radical transformation. Lily's initial response to memories of her mother is a need for forgiveness and absolution: "That night I lay in bed and thought about dying and going to be with my mother in paradise. I would meet her saying, 'Mother, forgive. Please forgive,' and she would kiss my skin till it grew chapped and tell me I was not to blame. She would tell me this for the first ten thousand years" (3).

Lily undergoes a roller coaster of emotions. The guilt and longing shift to denial and anger at the thought that Deborah would have left her. When Lily's fears are confirmed, her feelings shift to hatred. But when Lily learns that her mother married T. Ray because she was pregnant, the old guilt reemerges. Then, when Lily learns how much Deborah loved her newborn baby, she falls again back into the old pit of longing. Part of Lily's struggle with her mother is figuring out what to believe: Did her mother want her or not? Did she love Lily, or did she abandon Lily to an inadequate father?

While Lily begins needing forgiveness *from* her mother, she eventually finds she needs to offer forgiveness *to* her mother.

She recognizes the difficulty of this: "People, in general, would rather die than forgive. It's *that* hard. If God said in plain language, 'I'm giving you a choice, forgive or die,' a lot of people would go ahead and order their coffin" (277).

Understanding the importance of forgiveness is critical to understanding the message of Jesus Christ. In Matthew 6, Jesus teaches the disciples to petition God for forgiveness *and* acknowledge their forgiveness of others. Jesus repeatedly links God's willingness to forgive our failings, large and small, with an injunction that we forgive one another. In Matthew 18:21, Peter asks Jesus how many times he should forgive someone who sins against him, and Jesus responds, "seventy times seven." The figure is meant to indicate a number beyond our calculation.

Even though forgiveness is something we do "to" other people, the real recipient of forgiveness is ourselves. Refusal to forgive is a burden that we—not the other person—must bear. Even at her young age, Lily recognizes this: "In a weird way I must have loved my little collection of hurts and wounds. They provided me with some real nice sympathy, with the feeling I was exceptional. I was the girl abandoned by her mother. I was the girl who kneeled on grits. What a special case I was" (278).

As the novel concludes, Lily recognizes the plethora of "mothers" she has. Just as Jesus redefined family by making all followers his siblings, and making his biological mother the mother of the beloved disciple (see chap. 1), Lily learns to redefine family. The mothers she now has include those who love her, guide her, teach her, and nurture her.

Lily's "Baptism" into Her New Life

After Lily leaves the hateful wrath of T. Ray and hitches a ride toward Tiburon, she believes she has started a brand new life. The sacrament associated with new life is baptism. Baptism imagery is plentiful in *The Secret Life of Bees,* especially at points of transformation and reconciliation. Note how many critical changes involve water:

- Lily and Rosaleen bathe in a creek together the night after they flee Sylvan and after they argue about their plans. Lily awakes to what she considers the first day of her new life.

- A rainstorm on their first night at the Boatwright household is a time of renewal for Rosaleen, who "walked on puddles like they were Persian carpets… looked up at the drowned sky, opened her mouth, and let the rain fall in…Now I could see she was returning to herself, looking like an all-weather queen out there, like nothing could touch her" (75).

- When May crumbles emotionally upon hearing about a racist shooting in Georgia, a bath restores her.

- A water fight with a lawn sprinkler becomes the occasion of reconciliation between June and Lily.

- In drowning, May is given new life. According to Lily, "You could die in a river, but maybe you could get reborn in it, too, like the beehive tombs August had told me about" (229).

Baptism in the Bible

In the Bible, baptism is usually linked with the idea of repentance. Repentance is sometimes understood to mean feeling sorry for what you've done, or being punished. But a translation of the Greek word for repentance indicates something more like a change in perception or worldview. Christian baptism is ultimately about transformation, about starting a new life.

The Bible talks about baptism in two ways. The book of Acts tells a number of baptism stories, such as the story of

Lydia in Acts 16:13–15 and the story of a jailer who holds Paul and Silas captive in Acts 16:23–34. We also know about baptism from the letters of the apostle Paul.

Lydia is a faithful worshiper of God who, upon hearing Paul talk about Jesus, becomes a believer and is baptized along with all those in her home. She then opens her home to Paul and his companions and supports the new church in Philippi. While at Philippi, Paul and Silas are thrown in jail. A great earthquake opens the prison doors and breaks all the fetters, but Paul and Silas assure the jailer they have not escaped. (Such an escape would have brought severe punishment, even death, upon the jailer.) The jailer, whose name is not given, is so overcome he becomes a believer. He takes Paul and Silas into his home, tends their wounds, is baptized, feeds the guests, and lodges them for the night.

Some people understand baptism to be a requirement for salvation. But Paul's writings indicate that his main concern was that people lead ethical lives while they are still living. Paul wrote that we are buried with Jesus by baptism, "so that, just as Christ was raised from the dead…we too might walk in newness of life" (Rom. 6:4). His comments are surrounded by a lengthy discussion, not about going to heaven, but about how faithful Christians are supposed to live on Earth.

Baptism has many facets. One thing to remember is the activity of God in baptism. Throughout the biblical witness, divine forces draw people toward the act of baptism. Also, God is the main actor in baptism, effecting the change within the human heart that is signified in the baptism itself. Baptism is about being drawn into a community of believers, into Christian unity throughout the world. It is also about being drawn into close relationship with Jesus and being claimed as one of God's beloved children. As it relates to forgiveness of sins, baptism also signifies a break from a previous life and the start of a new life. As such, it is important to remember that baptism comes not at the end of the process of transformation, but at the beginning of a life of new beginnings.

Freedom, Forgiveness and New Life

Most of the baptism stories in the book of Acts go something like this: Someone hears the gospel proclaimed, believes, repents, is baptized in Jesus' name, and receives the Holy Spirit. (We might say that Lydia and the jailer demonstrates their gift of the Holy Spirit through their joyous generosity and concern for Paul's and Silas's well-being.) Paul, in his letter to the Romans, emphasizes an ethical life following baptism.

Lily never comments about her own baptism. As a Baptist in the South, it's likely she was not baptized as an infant. Lily regularly attends church with her father, and he could have encouraged Lily to get baptized. T. Ray, however, seems to ignore his daughter's spiritual needs. On the other hand, Lily is of an age where she could have been baptized, and we expect Brother Gerald would have strongly encouraged this; he may have even required it. But we don't know whether Lily underwent a traditional Baptist immersion baptism.

As *The Secret Life of Bees* is a story of religious alternatives, perhaps Kidd is using water images at times of transformation to demonstrate alternative baptisms: a baptism in a creek, a bath, a water fight, a rainstorm. Lily herself claims she is starting a new life, and this new life involves more than just a new place to live. But how does she express this?

Lily's embrace of a new life has a lot to do with coming to terms with her feelings about her mother. Their relationship hinges on the issue of forgiveness. Lily comes to realize that this forgiveness is less about whether Deborah failed as a mother, and more about Lily's own reliance on being hurt and abandoned. It is unclear, however, whether Lily comes to forgive either her mother or herself. As Lily grapples with the issue, she finds mouse bones, which come to symbolize her pain.

She cannot throw the bones away, but eventually has no need to carry them any longer. She sets them on a shelf: "I decided sometimes you just need to nurse something, that's all" (285).

The same evening, her mother is still on her mind: "Drifting off to sleep, I thought about her. How nobody is perfect. How you just have to close your eyes and breathe out and let the puzzle of the human heart be what it is" (285).

Life is indeed ambiguous, and the workings of the human heart mysterious. Lily finds an internal mother in Mary, and accepts the Daughters of Mary as her Earthly mothers. Were Lily a real teenager, we would hope that in addition to finding surrogate mothers, she would return to "the puzzle of the human heart" as she continues to mature. Forgiveness may prove to be a lifelong process. But when issues needing forgiveness are ignored, resentment, hurt, anger, and guilt are likely to hold a person captive to the past, preventing a full embrace of new life.

Fortunately, Lily is "wired" to seek God, especially in times of distress. It is also fortunate that Lily is receptive to a multitude of ways that God calls to her, since divine influences have their effect on Lily through nontraditional means.

God reaches into our lives in any number of ways to draw us closer, to each other and to God. With our ears attuned to the constant hum of grace, we are sure to find avenues to continuous renewal and growth.

QUESTIONS FOR DISCUSSION

1. Lily and Rosaleen sometimes refer to their life in the Boatwright household as a "dream world." Rosaleen thinks Lily needs to wake up from this world, but Lily wants to remain in it. Do you think that by the end of the novel Lily awakes from a "dream world"? Does her dream world become a real world?

2. In many novels the narrator is not the main character, but a commentator on the main character (as in John Irving's

A Prayer for Owen Meany). How do you think this story would be different if it were told from the perspective of Rosaleen? of August? of June?

3. How do you think August's talk with Lily about finding a "mother" within her helps her? Should Lily also try to find a "father" within herself? Why or why not?

4. Examine Lily's feelings toward her mother. Do you think her anger at her mother is justified? Is her guilt? her longing? Why or why not? Do you think she forgives her mother? What roles do substitute mothers play in Lily's life? Can such surrogate mothers adequately fill the place left by a birth mother's disappearance?

5. How do you understand the baptism imagery in this novel? In what ways does this imagery reflect the meaning of New Testament baptism? In what ways does it differ? In what ways do all the baptism images reflect some facet of truth?

FURTHER READING

Sue Monk Kidd, *Dance of the Dissident Daughter.* San Francisco: HarperCollins, 1996.

Kathleen Norris, *Amazing Grace: A Vocabulary of Faith.* New York: Riverhead Books, 1998.

Keith Watkins, ed. *Baptism and Belonging: A Resource for Christian Worship.* Prepared by the Division of Homeland Ministries. St. Louis: Chalice Press, 1991.

Lauren F. Winner, *Mudhouse Sabbath.* Brewster, Mass.: Paraclete Press, 2003.

CHAPTER 5

Queen
AUGUST'S COMMUNITY

On the second day, as they were drinking wine, the king again said to Esther, "What is your petition, Queen Esther? It shall be granted to you…" Then Queen Esther answered, "If I have won your favor, O king, and if it pleases the king, let my life be given me—that is my petition—and the lives of my people—that is my request. For we have been sold, I and my people, to be destroyed, to be killed, and to be annihilated."

(Esther 7:3–4a)

August closed her eyes, used her fingers to smooth out the skin on her forehead. I saw a shiny film across her eyes—the beginning of tears. Looking at her eyes, I could see a fire inside them. It was a hearth fire you could depend on, you could draw up to and get warm by if you were cold, or cook something on that would feed the emptiness in you. I felt like we were all adrift in the world, and all we had was the wet fire in August's eyes. But it was enough.

(Bees, 181)

"You're not Queen for a Day, you know." (*Bees*, 25)

After a night of kneeling painfully on uncooked grits, Lily awakes one morning to accusations from her father about sleeping late and shirking her duties at the peach stand. T. Ray takes her breakfast and feeds it to the dog.

Certainly, Lily is aware that she is *not* "Queen for a Day."

"Queen for a Day" was a radio, and later television, game show that ran from 1945 to 1964. It gave that dubious title, along with a velvet robe, crown, and scepter, to a female contestant who offered the most pathetic tale of her personal circumstances. The audience picked the winner from among several contestants by its applause, measured by an "applausemeter." As "Queen for a Day," the woman was showered with gifts such as appliances, furs, and jewelry. Instead of her dreary, hum-drum life, the woman would be given a day of rest and luxury (if the latest appliances could be called luxury), and called "Queen."

The show was criticized both in its day and today as exploitative of women in hard circumstances. Immediate material wants might be satisfied, but more enduring needs— including counseling or medical attention—were not addressed.

The Queen Bee

In common parlance, *queen* conveys an air of luxury, even idleness or aloofness. It implies a certain amount of privilege and removal from the day-to-day mediocrity that adorns most of our lives. If a woman behaves with great pomp and extravagance, or perhaps arrogance, we might say she's acting like the queen of Sheba.

But the term *queen* most likely does not imply a sense of power, authority, or responsibility. Nor does it include a sense of community; the woman is seen only in her role as it pertains to herself, although there might be a "let-them-eat-cake" attitude. The phrase *queen bee,* when applied to a woman within a group, does imply community and a certain degree of authority,

but perhaps not wisdom or duty. This is not the case in *The Secret Life of Bees.*

In previous chapters, we have looked mostly at women in their individual relationships with other women, such as Lily's relationship with her long-dead mother, or with her surrogate mother, Rosaleen. *The Secret Lives of Bees,* however, is largely about community. Lily leaves her place of isolation out on a peach farm to find the warm communal embrace of the calendar sisters and the Daughters of Mary. Rosaleen, who lived by herself, finds refuge and companionship in the Boatwright household. May, who on her own would have been doomed to life in an institution, is affirmed and given purpose in the company of her sisters and friends. In this chapter we will consider the idea of community. Because communities, including households, need leaders, we also will look at the role of "queen."

In *The Secret Life of Bees,* we learn that the role of a queen bee within a hive of worker bees is crucial. Without a queen, a group of bees becomes "completely demoralized" and die off. If the hive is not tended to carefully and the queen has no place to lay her eggs, there is a risk of a swarm. The queen bee's role is to lay the eggs: She is the mother of every bee in the hive. As such, she must be tended, not only by human caretakers, but by a group of attendant bees who groom and comfort her so that she can do her job. There must be a queen, but there can only be one.

In the Boatwright household, each woman plays a role in its smooth operation. In turn the household revolves around each of the women in a particular way: May's bent toward unquenchable sorrow is accommodated; the family tiptoes around June's relationship issues. The calendar sisters hover around Rosaleen, tending her wounds. When Lily faints or reflects on and adjusts to the news of her mother, the sisters hold her with care and tenderness. Within the community, each woman takes center stage as her need demands.

But the person orchestrating the entire household and its functioning is the eldest of the calendar sisters: August. We will consider August as the "queen bee" in the novel. She coordinates not only the household but also the honey operation and religious life. She offers guidance in everyday life as well. Like the queen of a beehive, August acts as mother in many ways to those who find their way to the bright pink house. She is most often the main "actor" in crisis situations, and she keeps the family history.

Through August's voice we hear not only the story of the Boatwright family but also the history of the black Mary that graces their parlor. Through August we learn about May, June, and Deborah. Beyond the circle of blood relatives, August is also the center of a larger community: the Daughters of Mary and the two men who spend a lot of time at the Boatwright place, Neil and Zach.

Forces of Wisdom: Queens in the Bible

Unlike our "Queen for a Day" example, queens in the Bible operate with a large degree of authority and power. Two biblical queens from the Old Testament are also recognized for wisdom.

The Queen of Sheba

Perhaps the most famous queen in the Bible is the queen of Sheba (1 Kings 10:1–13) who comes to Jerusalem to visit King Solomon. As noted in the introduction to this chapter, "queen of Sheba" can carry the connotation of opulence, and, indeed, the biblical queen was wealthy. She comes to Jerusalem from her home, most likely in southwest Arabia, with a "very great retinue" (v. 2), meaning she traveled in a great caravan or with a large company, or perhaps with great wealth. Camels bore gold and spices and precious stones. They also brought "almug wood" (vv. 11 and 12)—or sandalwood—used to build supports in the temple and in the king's house and to fashion musical instruments.

The queen of Sheba, having heard reports about Solomon's wisdom, comes to "test him with hard questions" (10:1). This may be a contest of wits, or perhaps she is seeking a display of Solomon's practical wisdom. She may pose certain riddles to test his brain power. Perhaps she simply seeks an exchange of ideas with a worthy conversation partner. The context of the conversation between the royals is left to our imaginations. Whatever the queen is seeking, she is duly impressed, not only with Solomon's mind but also with his house, his food, his servants, and his faith.

The queen of Sheba is not threatened by Solomon's success, nor does she seek a sexual encounter. Instead, she concludes their conversation with a blessing to his wives and servants and with admiration for the God of Israel. The two exchange gifts, and she returns to her own land. This queen lays claim to her own authority, her own power, and her own material wealth. She needs nothing from Solomon but an intellectual exchange. It should be pointed out that Ethiopian tradition holds that the queen of Sheba later gave birth to Solomon's child and that thus the Ethiopians can also claim a Davidic heritage. This tradition, however, is not in the Bible.

A Tale of Two Queens

Queen Esther, from the book of Esther, likewise uses her brain, as well as her beauty, to accomplish her goal. But unlike the queen of Sheba, Esther is not wealthy and powerful when she first appears in the Bible. Also, her actions arise out of concern for her community, the Jewish people.

The book of Esther is really the story of two queens: Vashti and Esther, each of whom is queen to King Ahasuerus. The story begins when the king throws a feast for the men, and Vashti throws a feast for the women. On the seventh day, when the king is good and drunk, he calls for Queen Vashti to appear in her royal crown so that people can see her beauty. She refuses.

The Bible doesn't tell us why Vashti won't appear before the king. Some believe the king's order implies that he wanted to display not just her beautiful face, but her beautiful body. In this case, Vashti is protecting her dignity and modesty by refusing to be paraded in a sexual manner before a group of drunken men. Others think Vashti refuses because the king, obviously drunk, is not making rational choices. At any rate, the king's advisers, in what some scholars believe is buffoonish exaggeration, imagine Vashti's actions will lead all women to disobey their husbands. Vashti has to be punished—and replaced.

An edict goes out to gather all the beautiful young women of marriageable age into the harem. After a year of undergoing beauty treatments, they will be brought to the king for a night, and he will choose the one he likes best to be his queen. The young women's feelings and desires are not consulted in this.

Among the women is Esther, a Jew. Orphaned as a child, she had been adopted by her cousin Mordecai. Mordecai tells Esther to keep her ethnicity a secret from Ahasuerus. Once taken in, Esther wins the favor of the chief eunuch, who helps her then win the favor of King Ahasuerus. The King makes Esther his queen, placing on her head the very crown that Vashti had refused to wear. Once a powerless orphan, Esther is now perhaps the most powerful woman in the kingdom.

Meanwhile, Mordecai angers the king's right-hand man, Haman, who subsequently plots to destroy the Jews. Haman tells the king the Jews are a "people scattered and separated among the peoples in all the provinces of your kingdom; their laws are different from those of every other people, and they do not keep the king's laws, so that it is not appropriate for the king to tolerate them" (3:8). An edict goes out that the Jews are to be destroyed.

Mordecai asks Esther to save her people. Esther initially declines, as approaching the king could mean her death. But she soon takes charge of the situation. In a remarkable use of social and royal strategy, Esther approaches the king and convinces him over a series of banquets to save the Jewish people. She also manages to bring about the downfall of Haman and the elevation of Mordecai. The Jews are saved through the slaughter of their enemies.

It is tempting to compare Vashti and Esther. Some scholars have found in Vashti a woman who resisted exploitation and in Esther a woman who let herself be exploited. But we need not set these two queens up as foils. We don't know why Vashti refused her husband, but we can imagine her refusal involved his drunkenness. We can take away from Vashti's story the ridiculous, exaggerated response by King Ahasuerus. As for Esther, we can admire her cleverness. She was no mere pawn, but intentionally positioned herself to make the best of a bad situation. In one sense, Esther wasn't exploited, but in fact used the male-dominated power structure to achieve her goal: saving the Jewish people.

If the story sounds cruel, remember that this book was written for Jewish people in a time of exile. They were an oppressed minority. This story wasn't meant to convey history, but to bring hope to a conquered people who had been pulled from their homeland. Sometimes in the Bible a single character may be meant to personify all of Israel. In this case, Israel may have seen itself as Esther, a people of humble beginnings who, through cleverness and strategy, create for themselves a situation of power and influence.

"Queen Bee" in *The Secret Life of Bees*

The story of Queen Esther is remembered during the observation of the Feast of Purim, which celebrates the Jews' deliverance from the enemies of the story. The feast may have begun during the diaspora, eventually becoming accepted in Judea. The main theme of the story is that Esther acted to save her community.

In *The Secret Life of Bees,* August is one distinct personality among many personalities in her community. Yet her specific role as the primary leader within the Boatwright household is crucial. Note how the other characters look to August for guidance or for approval and how she seeks ways to help each person live as fully as possible. Often August has the final say-so, even if the other characters appear to make decisions. As "queen bee," August leads her family and the Daughters of Mary. She leads in other ways as well:

- August is the primary actor in times of emergency. Although all the characters comfort and care for May, August responds the most strongly in the most extreme times of mourning. She leads the search for May and visits Zach in jail. The crisis leader demonstrates strength in the community.

- August is the holder of history. August gives voice to her family's history and to the history of the black Mary. For Lily, August also is the portal into the life and experience of her mother, Deborah. In relating the facts of history, the one who tells the story exercises power and assumes an important position.

- August is the religious leader. She not only leads the regular worship services but also is the spiritual guide for Lily and the other women, as well as the driving force behind the Daughters of Mary. The religious leader exercises pastoral care over her flock.

- August is the head of the honey operation. Although all the calendar sisters inherited the acreage on which they live, August is the businesswoman who makes the decisions and keeps the honey operation going. The financial leader creates stability for the others.

Being a "queen bee" is more than being in charge and telling people what to do. As "queen bee," August is responsible for her household's operation, for her sisters, and for her religious community. Remember that in the course of August's becoming an expert beekeeper, she has been stung hundreds, if not thousands, of times. Likewise, in opening her heart to the Daughters of Mary, Deborah, May, Lily, and the rest of those around her, August has opened herself to getting "stung" by disappointment and loss. The queen bee endures pain as she exercises power.

Queen in Community

Unlike contestants in "Queen for a Day," the biblical Esther and the fictional August seek to serve their peoples, not to be served. Both illustrate a woman acting as a leader of a community. For Esther, the concern is survival of her people. For August, the aim is that each member of her community be allowed to express him- or herself and to live life to the fullest.

The community that August serves and leads we know mostly through the observations of a girl who, at the outset, is an outsider. Before coming to the Boatwright household, Lily seems to have no sense of community, even though she lives with her father, attends school, and goes to church. Encouragement comes from a single teacher, and love comes from her housekeeper. No one else prods Lily to blossom, to dream, or to fulfill her dreams.

Consider what the term *community* means. We use the word to indicate a group of people living in the same physical or geographic area, such as a "retirement community" or a "resort community." The word sometimes means a group of people who share common interests or goals, such as "the business community" or "the art community." It can refer to a group of people who share a particular government, such as "the community of Springfield, Illinois." Or the term can indicate a group of people who share a cultural, ethnic, or historical heritage, such as "the African American community" or "the Jewish community." In each of these examples, the members of the group have something in common with one another. One characteristic of community is commonality.

But another characteristic of community has to do with difference. The members have something in common, but that very factor is often what distinguishes the group from the larger society. The business community exists in a world that is made up of many people who are *not* business people. The Jewish community exists within the larger secular world, as do the Islamic community and the Christian community.

When we think of the communities to which we belong—such as a church, a social or service fraternity, a family, or a country club—we sometimes think of the benefits that come with being part of a group. In community, we hope to find not only other people with whom we have something in common, but also members of that group who provide us with loyalty, encouragement, support, and mutuality.

Gradually Lily comes to feel integrated into her new community. A key turning point in her awareness happens after May's death, when Sugar-Girl references the foolishness of the drive-by window at the white funeral home. Her comment sends the Daughters of Mary into hysterical laughter.

> But I will tell you this secret thing, which not one of them saw, not even August, the thing that brought me the most cause for gladness. It was how Sugar-Girl said what she did, like I was truly one of them. Not one person in the room said, *Sugar-Girl,* really, *talking about white people like that and we have a white person present.* They didn't even think of me being different. (*Bees,* 208–9)

In this caring community, Lily flourishes. Her skinny figure begins to fill out. Her skills and interests are encouraged. Her personality is not threatened or squelched, but embraced and loved. Her spiritual and ethical life is tended to.

As the Daughters of Mary celebrate Mary Day, they rub honey into the statue. The movement of their hands forms a stirring metaphor for community:

Our lady was covered with hands, every shade of brown and black, going in their own directions, but then the strangest thing started happening. Gradually all our hands fell into the same movement, sliding up and down the statue in long, slow strokes, then changing to a sideways motion, like a flock of birds that shifts direction in the sky at the same moment, and you're left wondering who gave the order. (*Bees,* 270)

Most people are part of more than one community, and sometimes loyalties can conflict. When Zach and Lily drive into town on an errand, they come upon a standoff between a group of young black men and a group of older white men. When one of the black men throws a bottle that hits one of the white men, Lily desperately wants Zach to reveal the culprit rather than go to jail with the group. But Zach keeps quiet. As Lily interprets it, "He chose to stand there and be one of them" (179).

Over the course of *The Secret Life of Bees,* the Boatwright household gradually envelops Lily. Lily's adoption into the Daughters of Mary and into the Boatwright home may challenge our notions of what constitutes community. Although she is a white girl among older black women, she eventually feels accepted. What was it that Lily shared with this group?

Communities within Communities

A recent professional conference in a Southern city drew more than one hundred men and women from all over the country. They shared in common special interests, questions, concerns, and abilities. They ate some meals together, socialized with one another, and attended workshops together. At the close of the conference a group of about a dozen women gathered in a circle, held hands, bowed their heads, and prayed. In the name of Jesus, they thanked God for their conference experiences and asked God for safe travel to their various homes. They lifted up specific concerns some of the women had: family troubles, career troubles, health concerns. As the women gathered in that circle of praise and prayer, they were a community of Christians within a larger community of professionals.

Since the very first followers of Jesus gathered to learn, worship, and pray, Christians have existed as communities within communities. What they share in common—belief in Jesus as Christ—distinguishes them from the larger society.

Jesus' first, closest followers were Jews, as was Jesus himself. Of course, not all Jews believed that Jesus was the long-awaited messiah, and so those who did believe existed in two worlds. They were part of a community as followers of Jesus. They were also part of their larger cultural world of Judaism. Judaism was itself a minority community within the larger world of the Roman Empire.

Jesus drew followers from outside Judaism, too. Recall the Syrophoenecian mother we discussed in chapter 2. She was a Gentile, not a Jew. Another famous follower of Jesus, the woman at the well (Jn. 4:7–42), was a Samaritan. The Samaritans and Jews claimed a common ancestry, but by Jesus' time they were two distinct opposing peoples. From the days of Jesus, part of what has drawn Christians together has been differences, for Jesus called not only to his own people, the Jews, but to people of other ethnic groups, other social classes, as well as the marginalized and the socially despised.

In thinking about what makes up our "community within the community," we might find ourselves in the shoes of that lawyer who, in Luke 10:29, asks Jesus, "who is my neighbor?" Jesus responds to that question with the famous parable of the good Samaritan (Lk. 10:30–37). Christian community is based not on similarities of ethnicity or national origin, but on the love of God and one another despite differences.

Much of the book of Acts and the letters of people such as John and the apostle Paul take up the issue of how Christians are to behave as a "community within a community." It was difficult for the early churches, be they composed of Jewish Christians, Gentile Christians, or both. Not only did these communities need to discern what held them together, but also what distinguished them from the larger community in which they existed. Some needed convincing, particularly in situations of violent persecution by the majority authority, to remain in community.

In relatively modern times, some Christians have found themselves existing as a community within a larger world, and often against it. In the mid-1930s, during Hitler's rise to power in Germany, Dietrich Bonhoeffer received a call to lead an underground seminary for young ministers in Pomerania. Despite the constant Nazi threat, Bonhoeffer considered a common life with those dedicated to Christian ministry to be a gift. An outspoken critic of the Nazi regime, Bonhoeffer was executed in 1945 in the Flossenburg concentration camp, shortly before Allied forces liberated it. But his time in the "illegal" seminary led him to write eloquently and passionately about life in community. Bonhoeffer's *Life Together* describes the experience of drawing closer to God by living a common life with fellow Christians. He testifies to how we can only truly know one another through relationship with God.

It's Not Easy Being Queen

Consider all the women in leadership positions you know, or know of, be they political, religious, or business leaders, or agents of social change, such as those involved in the suffrage movement. Consider the leadership roles women take in family and church. What sacrifices have these women made? Have they made personal compromises? Have they had to sacrifice some aspect of personal security to serve a community?

Being "queen bee" means assuming responsibilities and duties beyond those we have for ourselves and for our families. As the traditional caretakers in the family, wives and mothers find themselves in sticky spots when they assume leadership roles. Especially in the political realm, it is not unusual for women leaders to be criticized for neglecting family duties or societal obligations or expectations.

Further, sometimes being "queen" requires a woman to do things she might prefer not to do. Recall the stories of August and Esther. Each may appear to readers to make personal compromises for the sake of the people whom they lead. Some may even think that August and Esther allow themselves to be exploited.

For example, Esther initially balks at the idea of approaching the king to save her people, as it puts her at great personal risk. But Mordecai responds:

> "Do not think that in the king's palace you will escape any more than all the other Jews. For if you keep silence at such a time as this, relief and deliverance will rise for the Jews from another quarter, but you and your father's family will perish. Who knows? Perhaps you have come to royal dignity for just such a time as this." (Esth. 4:13–14)

Queen Esther uses her charm and wit, acting in supplication to the king, to secure the safety of her people. The story of Esther gives us an illustration of a woman who perceives a real threat and must act on it, despite risk to her personal safety.

Esther's actions can in some ways be likened to the actions of August. For example, August tells Lily that when she couldn't get a teaching job, she kept house for a white family. Such a position would not have been palatable to June, who chose to work for a black-owned funeral home. Much later, in dealing with T. Ray, August chooses an indirect approach. Even though he bursts uninvited into her home, August talks in a consoling tone, letting him believe that he would be doing the Boatwright household a large favor by letting Lily stay on. We can only infer that August would have preferred not to keep house for a white family and would have preferred to blast T. Ray with sharp words.

Unlike the story of Esther, August's story makes it difficult to perceive a struggle in her person that would lead us to think she was acting against her own will. Nor do we perceive a threat to her personal safety. We might imagine that as a black woman she has faced discrimination and even threats. But the community that August has built and through which she nurtures its members seems secure. If August or her business are ever threatened, we readers are unaware of it. The crisis situations that August faces involve the personal crises of others: Lily's search for her mother, Sugar-Girl's ire at her husband, May's deep sorrow.

Without knowing August's personal struggles, in which her loyalties come into conflict, it is difficult to see how she might be a useful example when our own loyalties come into conflict. What are we to do when responsibility to our family comes into conflict with our personal career goals and duties? How do we simultaneously be leaders in our communities and take care of ourselves?

What we can find in August is the importance of having a strong, wise, and loyal leader on whom we can rely. Not only is she committed to serving her people, as is Esther, but August seeks to embrace each member of her community. She not only accepts their God-given particularities but also seeks to prod and encourage them to live the full, rich lives that God intends. This is the importance and gift of a healthy community. Being with others brings out our own distinct natures, which are gifts from God, and pushes us to use these gifts to their fullest.

QUESTIONS FOR DISCUSSION

1. August is both a queenly figure in *The Secret Life of Bees* and a mother figure. How are the two roles alike? How are they different?

2. List all the communities to which you belong. What benefits do they offer? Are there any costs to belonging to a group of people?

3. Consider all the women leaders you know, and imagine all the sacrifices they may have made. What are the qualities you appreciate in a good leader?

4. As "queen bee," how does August encourage those in her community to live fully? Are there ways in which she could do a better job? Consider how life in a community setting promotes, or prohibits, each member of the community's living as fully as possible.

FURTHER READING

Dietrich Bonhoeffer, *Life Together*. San Francisco: HarperSanFrancisco, 1978.

Fran Craddock, Martha Faw, and Nancy Heimer, *In the Fullness of Time: A History of Women in the Christian Church (Disciples of Christ)*. St. Louis: Chalice Press, 1999.

Richard J. Foster, *Streams of Living Water*. San Francisco: HarperSanFrancisco, 1998.

Robert D. Putnam and Lewis M. Feldstein, *Better Together*. New York: Simon & Schuster, 2003.

CHAPTER 6

Wife
DEBORAH'S CHOICES

A capable wife who can find?
  She is far more precious than jewels.
The heart of her husband trusts in her,
  and he will have no lack of gain.
 She does him good, and not harm,
  all the days of her life…
She considers a field and buys it;
  with the fruit of her hands she plants a vineyard.
She girds her loins with strength,
  and makes her arms strong…
She opens her mouth with wisdom,
  and the teaching of kindness is on her tongue.
She looks well to the ways of her household,
  and does not eat the bread of idleness.

(Prov. 31:10–27)

*The whole time we worked, I marveled at how mixed up
people got when it came to love.*

(*Bees*, 133)

When Lily hears about June's being jilted at the altar many years before, a thought occurs to her: "It struck me for the first time how odd it was that none of them were married. Three unmarried sisters living together like this" (103).

Because the Boatwright sisters are all single and because all but one of the Daughters of Mary are women, it is not surprising that *The Secret Life of Bees* revolves around relationships among women. Men are a minority in the novel, and man-woman relationships are, for the most part, in the periphery.

In previous chapters, we looked at a number of woman-to-woman relationships: sister-to-sister, mother-to-daughter, queen-to-community. In this chapter, as we look at the role of "wife," we open the question of love relationships between men and women. But we face a problem we have faced before. When we looked at mothers, we noted that the primary biological mother of the novel was absent. The same is true for the most prominent example of a wife, Deborah Fontanel Owens.

Deborah's case is a tragic one. Kidd, however, does not abandon the idea of healthy love relationships between men and women. While some woman-centered movies and books have been accused of "man-bashing" or failing to provide positive male characters (*Waiting to Exhale, The Color Purple, Thelma and Louise*), Kidd provides positive man-woman relationships, primarily in the relationship of June and Neil, turbulent though it may be, and in the budding love between Lily and Zach.

Ought vs. Is: Wives in the Bible

The Bible speaks of many subjects in two ways. It often gives rules or guidelines for behavior and understanding: "Remember the sabbath day and keep it holy" (Ex. 20:8); "You shall love the Lord your God with all your heart, and with all your soul, and with all your strength, and with all your mind; and your neighbor as yourself" (Lk. 10:27); "Do not worry about anything, but in everything by prayer and supplication with thanksgiving let your requests be made known to God" (Phil. 4:6).

The Bible also gives us narratives. These are stories and histories about what people actually did, or parables that people told. For example, Mark's gospel relates a story of Jesus' plucking heads of grain from a field on the sabbath, an act for which the Pharisees criticize him (Mk. 2:23–28). In answering a question about "who is my neighbor," Jesus tells the parable of the good Samaritan (Lk. 10:25–37). If we want to see an example of someone who is anxious, we can look again at the story of Mary and Martha (Lk. 10:38–42).

Likewise, the Bible discusses wives in two ways. We have guidelines, such as the partial quotation from Proverbs 31 and what we find in a number of epistles. We also have stories and histories of women. If you believe the Bible paints an oppressive picture of how a wife "ought" to behave, you might take note that many wives portrayed in the Bible are nothing like the often quoted guidelines.

How a wife "ought" to be. The book of Proverbs gives us a lengthy description of a "good wife" (RSV). There is no mention of her looks or her sexual appeal. Rather, the emphasis is on her industriousness, her generosity, her business sense, and mostly her hard work. The capable wife "rises while it is still night / and provides food for her household / and tasks for her servant girls" (31:15). But she also "opens her hand to the poor, / and reaches out her hands to the needy" (31:20). She dresses well and makes her husband and children proud. Proverbs also offers a number of ideas about how a woman or wife ought *not* to be: "A good wife is the crown of her husband, / but she who brings shame is like rottenness in his bones" (12:4); "A wife's quarreling is a continual dripping of rain" (19:13); "It is better to live in a corner of the housetop than in a house shared with a contentious wife" (21:9).

In the New Testament, our "guidelines" for how to be a good wife come in letters, two of which are attributed to the apostle Paul. Colossians states, "Wives, be subject to your husbands, as is fitting in the Lord." Importantly, the letter continues: "Husbands, love your wives and never treat them harshly" (Col. 3:18–19). Ephesians carries a similar message, using Christ's relationship with the church as a model for how a household ought to run: "Wives, be subject to your husbands as you are to the Lord. For the husband is the head of the wife just as Christ is the head of the church…Husbands, love your wives, just as Christ loved the church" (5:22–25). We could also look at 1 Peter 3:1–7 and Titus 2:3–5.

These passages are often described as "household codes." They give instruction for relationships, not just between husbands and wives, but between slaves and masters and parents and children. Portions of 1 Timothy, especially chapter 2, are also considered part of the rules for a Christian household.

These passages can be difficult for married women to swallow. Some people ignore or dismiss them as products of an ancient culture, the rules for which simply no longer apply. Other people believe that the whole Bible should be obeyed and that the call for submission on the part of wives is just as valid today as it was in the first century. They argue that a person of faith simply cannot "pick and choose" which parts of the Bible to follow.

It is important to put scriptures in their historical context. Much of the Bible was written during a time of systematic patriarchy that allowed slavery. Marriage was, in some ways, more about economics and security than it was about love. Social order was important (remember Queen Vashti from chap. 5). This was especially true for the Greek society in which Christianity was born. Religions that seemed to upset social order were viewed with suspicion. Christianity opened itself to such suspicion as it drew large numbers of slaves and women, whom society marginalized but who found acceptance and esteem in the Christian community.

New Testament writers often distinguished the behavior of church members from the behavior of the world at large, such as distribution of goods among the needy and social unity. At the same time, church leaders did not want to upset the apple cart or draw undue attention to the early church, especially during times of persecution. Early Christians did not want the ruling government to think it had anything to fear from this new religion. While Christians were supposed to have values and behaviors that were different from the world at large, they still had to live in the world at large.

Remember, too, that Paul wrote frequently about the equality of all baptized Christians: "There is no longer Jew or Greek, there is no longer slave or free, there is no longer male and female; for all of you are one in Christ Jesus" (Gal. 3:28). A number of scholars believe that Paul's earliest writings reflect that equality. The church, however, grew increasingly patriarchal with each passing decade, especially as Paul and the original apostles died off. Apparently, many of the household codes were recorded during this time.

If early Christians were supposed to maintain the culturally acceptable household practices of their time, we might ask, shouldn't Christians today do the same? Might that not mean that today's wives, who often share "breadwinner" and other household duties with their husbands, need not "be subject" to them, but in partnership with them? Or that men, understanding women's equal legal status in the broader culture, need not lay automatic claim to head status in the household?

In looking at the Colossians passage regarding husbands and wives, note the overall tone of mutuality. In considering passages of scripture that seem to go against our personal values and codes of conduct, as Christians it is always crucial to remember the overall message of Jesus: love for one another, care for the weak and needy, and equality of all people in the eyes of God.

Not always what she "ought" to be. Although the Bible sometimes offers instructions on how things *ought* to be, it also provides stories in which people's actions don't align with that ideal. The book of Proverbs describes an industrious, hardworking wife, without mention of her looks. Yet in the Old Testament, men frequently picked wives because of their good looks, as we might recall from the story of Rachel and Leah. The Song of Solomon, which some believe to be wedding poetry, conveys the deep physical, sexual attraction between a man and a woman who are very much in love.

We have already discussed a number of biblical wives, including Sarah/Sarai, Ruth, Naomi, and Mary, the mother of Jesus. The Bible shows us a number of other wives who do not always play by the rules. Lot's wife (whose name is not given) disobeys instructions from God's angels not to look back at the cities of Sodom and Gomorrah. God was to destroy the cities with sulfur and fire, and Lot and his family were to flee without looking back. Lot's wife does look back and is turned into a pillar of salt.

Later in Genesis, Joseph is a favored and successful member of Pharaoh's household. His good looks get the best of him, however, when the wife of Potiphar, one of pharaoh's officers, attempts to seduce him. Joseph resists the repeated advances of Potiphar's wife, who, like Lot's wife, is never named in the Bible. One day she grabs Joseph's garment, demanding he sleep with her. But he runs away, leaving the garment in her hand. She uses the garment as evidence to accuse Joseph of insulting her, and Joseph is thrown in prison.

In the New Testament, Sapphira acts with her husband, Ananias, to sell a piece of property. They withhold some of the proceeds from the early Christian community and then lie about the selling price. Both are struck dead (Acts 5:1–10). Herodias, the wife of Herod Antipas, acts on her own to engineer the beheading of John the Baptist. Herodias had been married to Herod Philip, with whom she had a daughter, known to historians as Salome. Herodias and Herod Philip divorced, and Herodias married her brother-in-law, Herod Antipas. John the Baptist spoke sharply against the marriage, saying it was "not lawful." Herodias, therefore, has it in for John. When Antipas asks to grant Salome any wish she desires, Herodias tells Salome to ask for the head of John the Baptist on a platter (Mt. 14:3–11; Mk. 6:17–28; Lk. 3).

David had a number of wives, both before and after his rise to the throne. The Bible says the first is Michal, the younger of King Saul's daughters. Saul takes young David into his household, but grows suspicious of the popular military hero. Saul is awestruck, but also angry and afraid. So Saul keeps David at battle, hoping he eventually will be killed. To ensure David's continued fighting, Saul offers Michal as a wife to "be a snare for him" (1 Sam. 18:21). As a "bride price," Saul asks for 100 foreskins of the Philistines, hoping David will die in battle. Michal loves David, as did all of Israel. David gets the foreskins and marries Michal, causing Saul to become all the more paranoid.

Michal's love for David prods her to help him escape Saul's murderous intentions and flee into the wilderness. In doing so, Michal cleverly tricks her father's soldiers, then boldly lies to her father, who no longer has her loyalty (19:11–17). While David is on the lam, Saul gives Michal to another man in marriage.

Meanwhile, David finds another wife in Abigail, the beautiful and intelligent wife of the boorish Nabal (1 Sam. 25:2–42). When Nabal refuses to help feed David and his followers, David is bent on revenge. But Abigail intercedes, bearing large quantities of food to David's men. She bows before David and, in an eloquent and strategically phrased speech, asks David to ignore her foolish husband. She convinces David that it would be a sin to seek retribution. David responds with blessing, admiring her intelligence and good will. He sends her home after agreeing to spare her household. When Nabal dies, David woos Abigail, and she agrees to marry him.

Michal's story, however, is not over. After King Saul dies, his house and David's house fight. David re-stakes his claim on

Michal, claiming he has paid the "bride price" (remember the foreskins?). It is merely a tactical maneuver. Well on the way to defeating Saul's house altogether, David reclaims his right to the King's house by taking back the king's daughter as his wife.

Michal's second husband weeps after her. Michal's sentiments are not recorded, but we might guess how she feels at being reclaimed by David, who is growing increasingly arrogant as he grows powerful. David soon becomes king over Judah and Israel and moves the capital to Jerusalem. There, "David took more concubines and wives" (2 Sam. 5:13). As he brings the ark of God into the capital city, "David dance[s] before the LORD with all his might; David [is] girded with a linen ephod" (6:14). This ephod was much like a loincloth, according to P. Kyle McCarter, Jr. (*The Anchor Bible,* vol. 9 [Garden City, N.Y.: Doubleday, 1984], 171). The scanty attire disgusts Michal, who watches his exaggerated, perhaps sexually suggestive dancing from her window. Where once she loved him, now she despises him (6:16).

Michal calls David to task, saying he has shamed himself "uncovering himself today before the eyes of this servants' maids, as any vulgar fellow might shamelessly uncover himself" (v. 20). David responds that God chose him over King Saul— Michal's father—and that he will do even more shameful things. The boy shepherd-turned-soldier whom Michael had fallen in love with is gone, leaving a boastful, arrogant king who acquires wives and concubines as he desires. Just five chapters later, David has an affair with Bathsheba and plots to have her husband killed.

As David has changed, so has Michal. Once a smitten bride willing to choose her new husband over her raving father king, she becomes a bitter woman who has been ripped from a husband who loved her and relocated in the house of an exhibitionist and arrogant king who refuses her children.

However, the Bible also gives us stories of faithful, loving relationships between husbands wives, such as Prisca (Priscilla), who works side-by-side with her husband, Aquila, to begin new Christian churches (see Acts 18:2, 18, 26 as well as references in Rom. 16:3; 1 Cor. 16:19; 2 Tim. 4:19).

Whether a "good wife" or not, each of the biblical wives noted throughout this book is her own woman. Not one submerges her personality or intelligence, but instead claims authority to act on her own.

Beyond Expectations: Women and Men in *The Secret Life of Bees*

Like many of the women in the Bible, women in *The Secret Life of Bees* act as individuals, not always following what family or society might expect, especially in matters of the heart. Each of the major characters bucks expectations according to what she believes to be best for herself. August, for example, refuses to consider marriage, seeing it as another potential "restriction" on her life.

Lily breaks "the rules" when she runs away from home, and then confounds even herself when she discovers her attraction to Zach. She confesses she had thought it would be impossible for a white girl to be attracted to a black man. "He had broad shoulders and a narrow waist and short-cropped hair like most of the Negro boys wore, but it was his face I couldn't help staring at. If he was shocked over me being white, I was shocked over him being handsome" (116).

The two begin as friends, but their gentle teasing turns to flirting. Lily finds herself fantasizing about him, despite the many reasons why such a relationship would be impossible; "maybe desire kicked in when it pleased without noticing the rules we lived and died by" (126).

Lily undergoes the usual stages of young love: roller-coaster emotions, vague anger, frustration, and unrelenting preoccupation. Unlike many smitten teenage girls, however, Lily never doubts her own worthiness. Many girls who become attracted to boys simultaneously begin to scrutinize themselves unfavorably. A girl might believe she is too fat, too smart, too ugly, too prudish. Lily, however, never questions her own adequacy in light of Zach.

Perhaps that is because the relationship is based on friendship with mutual encouragement. As Lily grows more attracted to Zach, she becomes more engrossed in her writing. Importantly, she also develops an appreciation for her body. Studying it in the mirror, she reflects: "It was the first time I'd felt like more than a scraggly girl" (134).

June confounds the expectations of all who are closest to her in her stubborn refusal to marry Neil, despite their lengthy courtship and his repeated proposals. Since she had been left at the altar so many years before, June has sworn not to marry. All the usual reasons for declining a marriage proposal are missing. The two are in love and available. Each has a good job. They have the backing of family and friends; in fact, Neil is almost a part of the Boatwright family already. What holds June back? August believes it is fear.

Midway through the novel, the relationship reaches a critical point: Neil proclaims he will "not wait around forever," but June claims she cannot marry him (123). In a final showdown in the tomato patch, each refuses to budge. Neil curses June as being "selfish" and leaves; June tells him not to return. Neil does return, however, at the point of an even larger crisis, Zach's arrest.

The stalemate might continue indefinitely were it not for May's suicide note, which urges the sisters to live life to the fullest. Prodded by August, June begins to consider the situation from a new perspective. Instead of marriage being surrender to the known and painful past rejection, perhaps in marrying Neil, June will be yielding to the unknown promises of the future. When Neil proposes again, the struggle remains. "June stared at Neil, and I could see the struggle in her face. The surrender she had to make inside. Not just to Neil but to life" (222).

We know **Deborah's** story through the memory of August. Deborah did not intend to go against societal expectations, but instead was eager to operate within them. Deborah wanted to marry. Although perhaps confused by her mixed feelings about T. Ray, Deborah wanted to be a wife and mother. She was willing to sacrifice her own desire to live in a town. Eventually, however, she realized she could not survive. Then she broke out of the norm by leaving T. Ray. In doing so, however, she defied her daughter's expectations of what a mother should be.

The tidbits of information we have about Deborah as a mother we collect throughout the novel from August, Lily, T. Ray, Rosaleen, and a couple of snapshots. But what we know about Deborah Fontanel Owens as a wife comes only at the end of the novel, and only from August. As a surrogate mother to Deborah, August regards Deborah's situation with deep compassion.

Deborah seems to have craved a loving, nurturing household, which we imagine she experienced under August's guiding hand. At 19, she had cried like a child when August moved to another city to take a teaching job. Just a few years later, Deborah moved to Sylvan, seeking the companionship of a girlfriend, the prospects of marriage, and the proximity to her beloved August.

It is not surprising, then, that she would have fallen for T. Ray, who doted on her and "treated her like a princess" (248). The time and culture in which Deborah and T. Ray lived encouraged them to get married. For Deborah, whatever charms T. Ray possessed rapidly wore off. She agreed to marriage anyway. We don't have any indication that T. Ray's feelings for Deborah changed before she left. Ultimately, his "worship" of her was insufficient to keep either of them happy. While T. Ray may have loved her still, it is possible that the expression of his feelings had changed. Certainly that expression changed *after* she left. August suggests that T. Ray himself changed.

We might put ourselves in T. Ray's shoes. As a decorated World War II veteran, T. Ray likely had broad experience overseas and had seen his share of danger. Just as Deborah felt the pressures of culture, T. Ray may also have felt pressure to put the ugliness of war behind him by confining himself to a peach orchard. Imagine his experience with the young, beautiful—and possibly sheltered and immature—Deborah. His dotings and affections were initially interpreted as true love, but soon Deborah, in her early twenties, came to be annoyed by small things such as dirt under the fingernails. When the love T. Ray felt for his bride ceased to be returned, bitterness may have encroached. Deborah had tried to make the marriage work, but could not. She became depressed, and T. Ray became bitter, and perhaps neglectful or abusive.

Perhaps it is the resemblance of Lily to the wife who abandoned him that makes T. Ray be so mean to her. As he stands in the Boatwright living room, his eyes "an ocean of hurt" (296), do you feel some compassion for him?

Following Her Own Heart

Lily wonders whether there were ever a time that August considered marriage. August responds, "I decided against marrying altogether. There were enough restrictions in my life without someone expecting me to wait on him hand and foot. Not that I'm against marrying, Lily. I'm just against how it's set up" (145).

As the Mary Day celebration wraps up, Otis and Sugar-Girl argue over her wig. Otis says she should not wear it; she wants to. The Daughters of Mary back her up. "Not because we *liked* her wig—it was the worst-looking thing you ever saw—we just didn't like Otis giving her orders" (267).

While *The Secret Life of Bees* gives us positive examples of male-female relationships, Kidd also makes it clear that women should claim their right to make decisions and act for themselves, even within a married relationship. For when a woman bows to societal expectations against her better judgment, she is bound to be unhappy, at best. At worst, and even against her intentions, her unhappiness will spread to her household, causing bitterness, anger, and resentment.

The Bible provides us with many examples of a wife who, within the structure of a marriage, maintains her own ideas and acts upon them, many times with benefit to a larger community. We've also seen in this book examples of women who are forced to submit to power structures (Jephthah's daughter, and Tamar), and wind up leading unhappy lives or dying prematurely.

The household codes of the ancient world have their correlation in strong and prevalent social expectations today. There was, and is, considerable pressure and expectation that a woman marry and produce children. Many women find deep satisfaction and happiness in marriage. Indeed, the family unit is crucial to the structure of our society, particularly in care and nurture of its most vulnerable members, such as children and the elderly. But even though structures and expectations are important, they can also be experienced as oppressive.

Bucking the system is difficult. Through the experience of Deborah Fontanel Owens, we learn what can happen when a woman simply goes along with expectations despite misgivings. Most of the main characters in *The Secret Life of Bees* find fulfillment when they refuse to play by the rules culture has set for them. In the end the novel gives us hope that as our society changes, "rules" that prevent people from realizing their full potential as human beings can be abandoned or changed. As Lily receives her first kiss from Zach, she wells up with a sense of optimism as she anticipates transformation: "Changes were coming, even to South Carolina—you could practically smell them in the air" (231). The immediate hope is for the cause of eradicating racism, but in a broader sense, it is a hope that oppressive structures of all sorts will be abandoned or transformed.

QUESTIONS FOR DISCUSSION

1. Does the Bible give us a negative or positive view of wives? How do you feel about using the Bible, written thousands of years ago, as a guideline for today's lifestyles?

2. When June and Neil fight, he accuses her of being "selfish" for wanting to remain single. Is he right? Why would choosing to remain single be a selfish act?

3. Deborah started out with positive feelings for T. Ray, but after a while the feelings "started wearing off." Why do some romantic feelings wear off, while others endure for decades? How do the romances described in *The Secret Life of Bees* differ from one another? How are they similar?

4. Consider the pressures involved with social and familial expectations. Could Deborah have *not* married T. Ray? What might her life have been like? What might Lily's life have been like?

FURTHER READING

Baruch Halpern. *David's Secret Demons*. Grand Rapids: Eerdmans, 2001.

Elisabeth Schüssler Fiorenza, *In Memory of Her*. New York: Herder & Herder, 1994.

Phyllis Trible, *God and the Rhetoric of Sexuality*. Philadelphia: Fortress Press, 1978.

Renita Weems, *I Asked for Intimacy*. San Diego: LuraMedia, 1993.